# The *Five*
## Great Principles
## *for* *Life*

# The *Five*
## *Great Principles*
## *for Life*

*Focus, Strength, Success, Wisdom, Responsibility*

## C. R. Stewart

**PELICAN PUBLISHING COMPANY**
GRETNA 2011

First published as The Window: Viewing the Essential Balance to
    Life and Success by Trafford Publishing, 2009
Published by arrangement with the author by
    Pelican Publishing Company, Inc., 2011

*The word "Pelican" and the depiction of a pelican
are trademarks of Pelican Publishing Company, Inc.,
and are registered in the U.S. Patent and Trademark Office.*

ISBN: 9781455615216
e-book ISBN: 9781455615223

Printed in the United States of America
Published by Pelican Publishing Company, Inc.
1000 Burmaster Street, Gretna, Louisiana 70053

*"A posse ad esse"*
*From possibility to actuality*

# Contents

Acknowledgements . . . . . . . . . . . . . . . . . . . . . . . . . . . . . . . vii
Introduction . . . . . . . . . . . . . . . . . . . . . . . . . . . . . . . . . . .ix
About the Author . . . . . . . . . . . . . . . . . . . . . . . . . . . . . . . .xi

## Focus

1   Raising the Bar. . . . . . . . . . . . . . . . . . . . . . . . . . . . . . 3
2   The Significance of Passion . . . . . . . . . . . . . . . . . . . . 11
3   Touching Your Potential. . . . . . . . . . . . . . . . . . . . . . . 16
4   Attitude Is Everything . . . . . . . . . . . . . . . . . . . . . . . . 23
5   No More Anchors . . . . . . . . . . . . . . . . . . . . . . . . . . . 28

## Strength

6   The Art of Discipline. . . . . . . . . . . . . . . . . . . . . . . . 37
7   Attack Your Weak Points . . . . . . . . . . . . . . . . . . . . . 41
8   Failure Is Not an Option . . . . . . . . . . . . . . . . . . . . . 46
9   Dictate to Events . . . . . . . . . . . . . . . . . . . . . . . . . . 52
10  No Excuses, Only Solutions. . . . . . . . . . . . . . . . . . . . 57

## Success

11  Moving Forward. . . . . . . . . . . . . . . . . . . . . . . . . . . . 63
12  Patient Determination . . . . . . . . . . . . . . . . . . . . . . . 68
13  Always Learning and Growing . . . . . . . . . . . . . . . . . 73

14 Flexibility and Adaptability . . . . . . . . . . . . . . . . . . . . . 78
15 Expect Change . . . . . . . . . . . . . . . . . . . . . . . . . . . . . . . 82
16 Be Prepared for Success . . . . . . . . . . . . . . . . . . . . . . . . 86

## Wisdom

17 The Essence of Rest . . . . . . . . . . . . . . . . . . . . . . . . . . . 93
18 Master Your Morning . . . . . . . . . . . . . . . . . . . . . . . . . . 96
19 Learn to Relax . . . . . . . . . . . . . . . . . . . . . . . . . . . . . . 100
20 This is the Best Time of Your Life . . . . . . . . . . . . . . . 103
21 Giving and Receiving . . . . . . . . . . . . . . . . . . . . . . . . . 107
22 Seizing Rare Moments . . . . . . . . . . . . . . . . . . . . . . . . 113
23 The Power of Simplicity . . . . . . . . . . . . . . . . . . . . . . . 117

## Responsibility

24 Leading Others . . . . . . . . . . . . . . . . . . . . . . . . . . . . . 123
25 Facing the Truth . . . . . . . . . . . . . . . . . . . . . . . . . . . . 129
26 You Are What You Eat . . . . . . . . . . . . . . . . . . . . . . . . 133
27 The Necessity of Physical Activity . . . . . . . . . . . . . . . 137

**Workbook** . . . . . . . . . . . . . . . . . . . . . . . . . . . . . . . . . . . **141**

# *Acknowledgements*

I wish to express my heartfelt gratitude to two important people who made this endeavor possible and offered their overwhelming support through the process.

My mother, Barbara Stewart, whose encouragement and love provided me with the guidance and commitment I needed. Her continual acts of kindness and devotion inspired me to write this book.

Pam Drouin, who has helped me work on my ideas, read through several drafts, and offered important insight and feedback through the entire process. Her wisdom, affection, and laughter made the journey truly enjoyable.

I would also like to thank my editor, Doris Pike, who assisted with the structure and flow of the entire book. She added great suggestions and helpful insights.

Thank you again.

# *Introduction*

I wrote *The Window* because I wanted to share essential principles about success I have learned over the last twenty years, concepts that will help others find genuine balance and achievement in life. Success is a multidimensional word, and while many books on the subject promise get-rich-quick fixes and try to sell their ideas about positive thinking, they do not offer realistic insight or examples that can carry someone forward. They promote certain steps or just inspire for a moment, but this is not enough. Yes, an optimistic attitude and staying focused on your goals are imperative, but there are many other issues and obstacles that happen along the way, as well as problems or beliefs that one may be dealing with or need to overcome, that these books do not address.

Succeeding at any objective takes time and commitment. Anything of value is not attained overnight, but will come by remaining diligent, confident, and driven. Despite your past or current situation, you have the ability to choose the direction you want to go in—and you can change that course in a minute. You can achieve what you want if you do not allow yourself to get sidetracked or discouraged. Your attitude and beliefs are vital in fostering results and living to your fullest. Only your determination and resolve will overcome trials and disappointments. While having money to do what you want is important, living life with passion and achieving your goals is essential. You need to realign yourself with what you really want, move in that direction, and work at accomplishing it—and this book will help you do just that.

The *Window* not only provides important principles for achieving your ambitions, but deals with these issues in a simple way, offering realistic insight and tying in relevant stories. It provides insight into tackling issues and moving through difficult problems. In a straightforward, concise language, it offers valuable ideas one may relate to and connect with in a powerful way. Many of the chapters discuss important truths that we know, but need to be remembered and practiced. Others offer examples of the fundamental principles to achievement and balance. Hopefully you will find the book encouraging, thought-provoking, and helpful. As you read through, take your time and reflect on each chapter. I have provided a workbook in the back that will help you navigate through issues, focus your goals, and put together a plan to achieve them. No matter what decade or century we live in, the concepts I have learned and shared are the same for everyone.

# About the Author

C. R. Stewart grew up in Newport Beach, California, and has spent the last twenty years gaining a comprehensive background in business, education, and human development. He has studied with over fifty professional trainers, coaches, and tutors, some of whom are renowned in their field. The one-on-one experience gave him the knowledge and discipline to learn subjects quickly, overcome difficult obstacles, and achieve continuous success. He has worked for three self-made millionaires, where he learned about business, entrepreneurship, setbacks, and accomplishment. He started his own company at age twenty and ran it for four years, before moving to New England, where he graduated from Brown University, and pursued his MBA at Boston College. He has spent years traveling around the world, studying diverse cultures and international business. He has worked for three Fortune 100 companies, and launched *The Britfield Group* at age 28 (**www. TheBritfieldGroup.com**), now an international consulting firm specializing in leadership, personal development, executive strategy, and knowledge enhancement. He works with clients and companies to help them elevate their expectations and maximize their success. He has been engaged in public speaking for over two decades and is now incorporating this book into lectures, workshops, and business engagements. He states, "*I found in life that if you are ever going to do something, you do it well or not at all. I do not believe that anyone should ever compromise their life or what they believe in.*"

# *Focus*

1  *Raising the Bar*
2  *The Significance of Passion*
3  *Touching Your Potential*
4  *Attitude Is Everything*
5  *No More Anchors*

# 1

# *Raising the Bar*

*"Great spirits have always encountered violent opposition from mediocre minds."* – Albert Einstein

Regardless of our accomplishments or failures in life, realize that we can never raise the bar high enough nor expect enough from ourselves, for we all possess astonishing talent and a capacity for greatness. Whether the simplest tasks or the most profound goals, we need to recognize our ability and tap what is inside us. Often, greatness is just one inch away, but fear and lack of confidence in ourselves render us powerless. With great expectations comes the opportunity to realize them. By desiring more, we create the capacity to receive it. By pushing ourselves harder, we can go further than imagined. In truth, most of us are at about 25 percent of our real potential or talent. Our true ability has been diverted to random acts of complacency and boredom. John Wooden wrote, *"Don't measure yourself by what you have accomplished, but by what you should have accomplished with your ability."* Whether privileged or deprived, we were not predestined at birth for mediocrity or an average life, yet most people accept it. They settled for something far less then what they could have been. Often just one setback or negative thought can divert our lives in the wrong direction. It becomes what we should have done, not what we did.

Our potential should never be about where we came from or have gone through. You may not have had the perfect upbringing, encouraging experiences, or the right education. You may be miles away from where you once wanted to be. Yet that should not preclude you from doing extraordinary things by reaching deep inside yourself to unearth your gifts and talents, which when used properly, can produce powerful results. Although past experiences can have a harsh effect on our current lives, we should put the past behind us; channel our minds toward where we are right now, and where we should go from here. Sri Chinmoy wrote, "*An uninspiring person believes according to what he achieves. An aspiring person achieves according to what he believes.*" Perhaps we chose a career based on what others wanted or what we believed felt safe at the time; we made decisions based on the wrong reasons. Perhaps we allowed one negative comment to rob us of our confidence. Anything can happen, but what we do about it now makes the difference. Do we choose to be the victim of circumstances or the author of our life? It is time to set the bar higher and create a compelling vision for the future.

The mind believes only what we allow it to accept, and reacts only to how it has been conditioned. Our beliefs are those we have formed. Whether right or wrong, it is the system we act on, but it is never too late to change. Henry Ford wrote, "*Whether you think you can or think you can't, you're right.*" Whatever we link to an incident or idea is what it becomes. Although some of our past events may be great memories or foster confidence, others work against us, limiting our talents and skills. Whether it was a college you never attended, a position you were passed over for, or a career that you never started, these circumstances are in the past. Whatever the situation, we have the power to change our lives in an instant. With just one new idea, we can alter our direction and transform our destiny.

Although a present situation or environment may not be beneficial, we can change it; and when you set a new goal or ambition, reach farther than seems possible.   Stewart B. Johnson wrote, *"Our business in life is not to get ahead of others but to get ahead of ourselves—to break our own records, to outstrip our yesterdays by our today."* If there is no limit to what a single person can accomplish, why limit ourselves.  With this attitude and perception, we can accomplish our greatest hopes; but we need to dream them first.  We must have the confidence to create the capacity to see it as well as accept the knowledge and understanding that anything is achievable.

> **Beliefs:**  Every decision we make in life is based on our beliefs.  Every conversation, relationship, and situation is measured and judged by what we believe.  Our past experiences influence and define our attitude.  Our personality, expectations, and how we treat others stems from this mindset.  Many beliefs encourage us to move forward, while others are debilitating and compromise everything we do. Often based on generalizations and misconceptions, they undermine our behavior and the decisions we make.  Whether a difficult childhood, bad experiences, or past failures, negative impressions can program our mind to believe these as truths and accept them as fact.  They set specific standards and patterns in our life, form certain limitations, and hinder us from accomplishing what we want.  Some debilitating beliefs are so ingrained in our mind that they form destructive patterns and negatively influence the rest of our lives.  Our generalizations become the basis for our present and future decisions.  But the past is just that—the past, a moment in time, many best forgotten.  In the present and the future, we

have the power to choose what we want and to make our life better by adjusting some of our beliefs.

Take time to ask yourself honest questions. Are your decisions and actions always right? Are they based on past experiences or what the future could hold; on your limitations or your expectations; what someone else said or what you know is possible? Do you truly feel that these assumptions are correct? Can you change some of these beliefs to improve your life? This self examination will undoubtedly reveal to you that past experiences should not always determine your future. Every moment offers a new chance to change and grow. Start asking better questions about your beliefs. By doing so, you will disrupt negative patterns with positive associations. Find the good in others and expect more from yourself. If we believe in achieving something, we will move forward. If we treat others with respect, we receive it back. Most of the greatest accomplishments in life started as impossibilities. Someone saw what could be done and did it; not because they were geniuses, but because they connected with the belief they could do it and continued until it was done.

Still, it is easy to get caught in a rut or even a comfort zone. You may have already achieved success or accomplished many goals, but this, too, can be limiting. You may confidently reflect on past achievements, but with so much capacity for growth and untapped talent, these successes are merely the beginning. Your potential is limitless. Even if you have been moving in a certain direction for years or think this is your best, there still remains far more inside you, areas you have not even touched on. We are all born with the potential to have impact in this world, a purpose even beyond ourselves. This capacity is within us. The possibility for growth is waiting to be unleashed. But we need to challenge ourselves and set higher expectations; clear our minds, think about it, and reflect on what it is we really want. Charles Colton wrote, "*Great minds must be ready not only to take opportunities, but to make them.*" Understand that the mind, when properly aligned with an objective or goal, can push us forward in a way never experienced before. With a determined will to achieve something, nothing can really stop it. Having bold vision propels us forward and provides us with the will to accomplish what seems impossible. But we need to realize this, see beyond the moment, visualize the future, and stop being our own worst opponent.

Be clear about what you want and understand why. Establishing the reasons for your goals helps you connect with them and offers a powerful reason to continue. Once you form these ambitions in your mind, write them down and create a plan for completing them. Put enthusiasm behind your thoughts and hold nothing back. If we aim low, we hit low; but by aiming higher, we position our lives in that direction. Know that there is power in boldness. Crush discouragement with confidence and defeat adversity with passion. When you know your direction and have formed some powerful objectives, surround yourself with the type of people that support you. We need to be built up, not torn down; pushed forward, not dragged back. Arnold Glasow wrote, "*A true friend never gets in your way unless you happen to be going down.*" We should all have at least one other person in our lives that keeps up on track and creates accountability; someone who is honest, but encouraging, who understands our potential and helps foster it. Johann Wolfgang von Goethe wrote, "*If I treat you as though you are what you are capable of becoming, I help you become that.*"

Regardless of your age or position, you can change your direction or destiny anytime. Retirement is a fable created by the unambitious. George Elliot wrote, "*It is never too late to become what you could have been.*" There is always time to pursue what you really want and to expect more out of yourself. At any moment, you can connect with an idea or dream and realize it. You have the power to choose this, and the ability to make your own decisions. You may not achieve your goal overnight; but begin it, and never allow circumstances or excuses to dictate the outcome. Abraham Lincoln wrote, *"A goal properly set is halfway reached."* Spend the time searching inside yourself and find what you really want to accomplish, what other ambitions are left unfinished. Dig deep and become excited at what you uncover. Edgar F. Roberts wrote, *"Every human mind is a great slumbering power until awakened by keen desire and by definite resolution to do."* We all need to have dare-to-be great moments, challenges bigger than ourselves, and something that stretches us and requires all our ability. Whether it is a great feat in your life or career; or, perhaps, something spectacular still not realized, dream it so you can accomplish it. With confident drive and focus, a person can achieve more in a week than they had in an entire month or, even, a year before. That is the power within all of us. Remember to raise the bar and set your standards higher.

I heard this true story of Walt Disney years ago. It impacted me that such an extraordinary man and a global business was founded by someone with no connections or money—just determination. His continual struggle and years of poverty left a profound impression on me. Although he is known for the characters he invented, Walt Disney was a man of real character, a visionary who set high standards, never gave up, and realized his goals.

# *Imagination*

Although the name Walt Disney is recognized throughout the world, his earlier life was anything but magical or successful. Born in 1901, Walter Elias Disney grew up with a creative passion for drawing and spent hours sketching figures on his barn walls, for which he was severely punished. After moving to Chicago and taking art classes, he became a cartoonist for the school newspaper. He left school early and moved to Kansas City, where he learned animation and decided to open his first company. Although his locale cartoons and ads were popular, he was soon in debt and the company filed bankruptcy. Searching for other opportunities, Disney moved to Hollywood, California. He went door to door with his sketch books, but no one was interested. After months of rejection, he decided to start another company. Progress was slow, and Disney spent five more years struggling with debt and poverty. By 1928, Disney finally had some success with a few of his cartoons, but he soon lost the rights to the characters. On hearing the news, most of his animation staff left for other companies. Disney was once again at the beginning. Desperate for a new character, he decided to sketch a drawing of a mouse and named him Mickey.

After a few silent animated shorts, Disney added sound to his next project: *Steamboat Willie*. It was an instant success and Mickey became the most popular cartoon character at the time. With his profits, his studio grew, and he hired the best innovators and animators in the business. In 1934, he began plans for the first full-length animated feature. The industry believed his ambitious project would fail and destroy his studio. They were nearly right. Spending years on perfecting the film, Disney finally ran out of money. At the last minute, he got a loan to finish the project, and the feature went on to become the most successful motion picture of 1938. His studio flourished and by 1950, Disney entered television and started hosting weekly series. In 1955, after five years of setbacks and cost overruns, Disney successfully opened his first amusement park, Disneyland. Although he died in 1966, his plans for Disney World and EPCOT were seen through by his brother, and the Disney Empire became the world's leading producer of family entertainment. As of today, The Walt Disney Company owns five vacation resorts, eleven theme parks, two water parks, thirty-nine hotels, eight motion picture studios, six record labels, and eleven cable television networks. By 2007, the company's annual revenue was over U.S. $35 billion. All this was created from one man's dream and vision.

# *Raising the Bar*

### Key Concepts and Focus

- We can never raise the bar high enough.
- Have the courage and confidence to get more out of life.
- Never settle for mediocrity and know that you are worth more.
- Reaching for greater things increases our capacity to receive them.
- Set higher standards and expect more from yourself daily.

# 2
## The Significance of Passion

*"Nothing great in the world has been accomplished without passion."* –Friedrich Hegel

Passion is an extraordinary and inescapable necessity of life—a quality that compels and drives us forward. It can provide us with the enthusiasm and power to endure the hardest of times and the ability to accomplish astonishing achievements. Everyone has this quality inside—a profound yet real emotion that, when connected, moves the mind and body symbiotically to create a dynamic and fulfilling life. Passion is the powerful facilitator behind thoughts and actions. It can inspire moments of great insight, provide daily guidance, and give life purpose. Earl Nightingale wrote, *"The more intensely we feel about an idea or a goal, the more assuredly the idea ... will direct us along the path to its fulfillment."* Anything is possible when you are passionate: a new job, a career, a wonderful relationship or an impossible goal. But we need to connect or reconnect with it. Find what is inside us: that joy, brilliance, and excitement for life. Yet, often it is not that easy. Life is a journey with innumerable, unexpected twists and turns.

Everyone experiences times of hardship, disappointment, or major setbacks. Events overwhelm us, and we eventually lose our passion for life. We allow mediocrity to sink in and circumstances to dictate us. We lose that childlike splendor and exciting creativity for the future—how quickly one negative thought or event can defuse our momentum. It can feel like the wind has been removed from our sails and we are just drifting at sea. Complacency sets in, doubt takes over, and we may not even be aware of it. One moment we are moving with power and enthusiasm, the next we are in the desert trying to figure out how we got there. Uncertainty creeps in and debilitates our potential, robbing us of what is really important. This happens with careers, friends, relationships, and life in general. Yet passion is one of the most valuable incentives for everything we do or pursue—the one common trait that most successful people have and the thread that ties everything together.

The dictionary describes passion as *an intense emotion that compels us forward, a strong desire and enthusiasm for something we want.* Even if it has been lost or compromised, we can get it back and must. One way is by direct action: Make passion a priority. Reconnect with what you love and enjoy. Learn to focus on the things you want and how you desire your life to be, not on your problems or failures. Where your focus is your mind will follow. Arnold Toynbee wrote, *"Apathy can only be overcome by enthusiasm, and enthusiasm can only be aroused by two things: first, an ideal which takes the imagination by storm, and second, a definite intelligible plan for carrying that ideal into practice."* Passion is a current always running through our lives; but we need to reach out and seize it, embrace it, protect it, and build on it. If you truly want to succeed, accomplish extraordinary feats, form strong relationships, and build a powerful future, passion is your catalyst. With passion comes initiative and self motivation, qualities critical for achieving your potential.

In the *7 Attributes to Success*, passion is the most important principle. Without it, there is no balance or powerful force behind what we accomplish. Those who succeed in life are driven by their passion and their love for what they do. Even in the face of trials and adversities, passion pushes us forward. We must never waiver from what we enjoy doing and what truly fulfills us. We must harness the power that ignites our desire, and let nothing stand in the way. Find what you enjoy in life, and the rest will follow; work at something that brings you satisfaction and everything else will come. Arthur Buddhold wrote, *"Follow your passion, and success will follow you."* Perhaps it is time to reconnect with an old friend, pursue a subject you once enjoyed, get involved in a sport, or fire up a relationship. Start today. Procrastination leads only to defeat. You may need to balance obligations with your pursuits, but never give up on what you are passionate about. We must embrace it and trust in its guidance. It will provide strength and perseverance, help us overcome difficulties, find solutions to problems, and realize our greatest goals. Passion can enlighten our mind, bring forth opportunity, and enable us to realize our true potential.

Love is the most powerful passion there is, for what we do and for those we care about. It has an extraordinary ability to take away fear, heal the soul, erase hardships, and restore the human spirit. The following story is a classic example of how life can be turned around and made into something truly wonderful with a passion for love.

## *A Passion for Love*

She was a forty-year-old invalid, physically confined to an upstairs room in her father's house. Her frailty and father's strict refusal to allow any of his eleven children to marry left her with little strength or hope for a better life. But she had a passion for writing poems filled will enthusiasm, excitement, and love. One day she received a letter from a younger man who read a few of her published verses and was deeply touched by the tenderness and passion conveyed through her writing. He was not only deeply moved by her poems, but by the poet herself. Her encouraging reply to the letter led to their first meeting; and after months of correspondence, they eventually fell in love. As he frequently visited her house, she found the strength to move from the confining upstairs room to the downstairs and eventually to the outside garden where they walked together for hours. That May, the two eloped to Italy and were happily married for fifteen years until she passed away in his arms. Her name was Elizabeth Barrett Browning, and her husband, the famous poet, Robert Browning. Inspired by her new found love and the passion she rediscovered for life, she wrote this famous poem for Robert:

# Sonnet 43

*How do I love thee? Let me count the ways.*
*I love thee to the depth and breadth and height*
*My soul can reach, when feeling out of sight*
*For the ends of Being and ideal Grace.*
*I love thee to the level of everyday's*
*Most quiet need, by sun and candle-light.*
*I love thee freely, as men strive for Right;*
*I love thee purely, as they turn from Praise.*
*I love thee with the passion put to use*
*In my old grief's, and with my childhood's faith.*
*I love thee with a love I seemed to lose*
*With my lost saints, -I love thee with the breath,*
*Smiles, tears, of all my life! – and, if God choose,*
*I shall but love thee better after death.*

# The Importance of Passion

## Key Concepts and Focus

- Passion is an inescapable necessity of life.
- The stronger your passion, the greater the results.
- It is a powerful characteristic behind achievement and success.
- Make a list of things you are passionate about and love doing.
- Plan this week to do at least one, and continue with it.
- Find others who share your desires and get them involved.

# 3

# *Touching Your Potential*

*"One person can completely change the character of a country, and the industry of its people, by dropping a single seed in fertile soil."* – John C. Gifford

Regardless of your past or current situation in life, everyone has a unique capacity to accomplish extraordinary goals and ambitions. Whether these ambitions are small or large, we all possess the profound ability to create our own life and guide it. Everyone has special talents and gifts waiting to be utilized, yet few realize or ever discover their true potential and believe in it. Many have learned to settle for mediocrity, allowed their hopes to be crushed, and lost their faith in people and themselves. We all have unlimited ability if only we can take time to clear our minds and connect with it. But too often we get distracted. Whether we are in the wrong career, a bad relationship, a negative environment, or a situation where we are being put down by others—these are all irrelevant to what is truly inside us. Never submit to them or allow them to overtake you. Werner Erhard wrote, *"Create your future from your future, not your past."* The greatest injustice we can do to ourselves is to limit our objectives, to lower our standards and expectations, or allow our past or current circumstances to dictate to us.

While a few people have more natural ability or can move faster, it does not make them better or the results more profound. Some have had advantages and opportunities, but it often detracts from their character. On the other hand, starting with modest means can offer us more strength of character. It is through the process that we develop and become stronger. Connections can help, but they do not make the difference. Thousands of great companies have been founded and built by those with no money or education. These visionaries just had a tenacity to succeed and found a way. The prevailing theory about the right genetics or biological combination is only myth and has no real impact on one's ability. In learning and knowledge development, it contributes only about 30% to the overall results and often has no real advantage, especially in adulthood. What does this mean? When you remove the excuses and discouraging conceptions that society has accepted, the fact remains that you can do anything you put your mind to; you can accomplish anything you want. There is no reason ever to settle for something less. Norman Vincent Peale wrote, "*No matter how dark things seem to be or actually are, raise your sights and see possibilities-always see them, for they're always there.*" It may take time to readjust your focus and ambitions, but it will come with practice and consistency. Many successful individuals worked for years or even decades to reach their objectives—but they did it. They expect more from themselves and got it.

Whatever the goal, by clearly connecting with it, we program our mind into acknowledging this as a reality—something we can accomplish. The more we believe in ourselves and concentrate on our ambitions, the more we increase the opportunity to realize them. Ralph Waldo Emerson wrote, "*Without ambition one starts nothing. Without work one finishes nothing. The prize will not be sent to you. You have to win it.*" The human mind is formed in such a way that we have the personal aptitude to direct our thoughts into powerful actions. By continuing to reflect on what we desire, we program our mind into helping us get there. It really is that easy, for your thoughts do become the life you create. In *The Seven Tenants of the Brain,* motivation and concentration are key factors for stimulating the mind and achieving powerful results. Other research on the brain's capacity shows that connecting your emotional focus with the willingness and attitude to achieve something fosters the drive to realizing it—an association your mind holds on to. The more willing and focused you are, the greater the success. But we must have the vision to see what we really want. Frank L. Gains wrote, "*Only he who can see the invisible can do the impossible.*

> **Words:** The words we use have the power either to inspire and motivate or discourage and debilitate. One negative word can have a profound effect on our behavior and attitude. For example, consider how the following words make us feel: *paycheck/taxes, bonus/layoffs, Saturday/Monday, success/failure, wealth/poverty.* In each, the first inspires us, and the second is demoralizing or, at best, unpleasant, demonstrating how just one word can suddenly alter our mood and change our outlook. Half the words in our vocabulary are negative. Using these has become part of our daily routine and manifests more problems in our lives; but we can change this. We can choose our vocabulary. Replacing negative words can break old patterns and modify our attitude. By concentrating on different words, we can instantly transform our behavior. Daily motivation and success depend on the language we use and what we tell ourselves.

> Affirmations are nothing more than the words we repeat in our mind. They are sentences we say out loud or thoughts we go over. Athletes use these before a game or performers before an event. If

you focus on your lack of confidence or repeat that something will never work, then your behavior follows that direction. However, if you consistently affirm that you will win, excel, or have a successful day, you open your mind to these possibilities and opportunities. The Navy Seals incorporated this psychology into their training program. Referred to as *"Self Talk,"* it represents the verbal motivation candidates tell themselves throughout the program. It makes the difference between those that complete the grueling training (about six-to-seven percent) and those that fail. Words and thoughts are like a compass. They set our direction and guide our life. Whatever you focus on, you attract back to yourself. Every thought we have causes a direct result in our lives.

Understand that most objectives are not obtained quickly, which make them worth more. Time can add value to what we desire. It is through the process of working toward our goals diligently that we mature and prepare ourselves for obtaining them. We condition our life to success—mentally, emotionally and physically. Our resolve and determination grow, forging an attitude of confidence and certainty. Few successful people have ever gained achievement overnight. We read only about their immediate results and not the years of hard work and effort. Many great entrepreneurs struggled for decades before they found the right combination and realized success. History is filled with ambitious people who finally achieved recognition only after years of repeated failures. Napoleon Hill wrote, *"Most great people have attained their greatest success just one step beyond their greatest failure."* Countless others have experienced incredible accomplishments because they recognized what was inside them, what they wanted out of life, and never gave up until they had it. Amazing things can happen when you are not affected by obstacles or setbacks.

Even if you have moved out into the world and achieved what many deem as success, you still have not even touched your potential. There is no real ceiling to it; only the one we construct. Edward Young wrote, "*They build too low who build beneath the skies.*" That is truly what makes life extraordinary if only you embrace it. Never allow excuses to distract you from what is really inside you; what you really want out of life. Young also warned us that "*Procrastination is the thief of time.*" If you want to write a book, pick a subject (preferably something you know), form an outline, research the theme, and write. If you want to start a company, figure out what you are passionate about, put together a business plan, form an alliance of insightful people, and start. If you have always wanted to be a professor, an architect, a doctor, or whatever profession, research the topic, find the right school, work hard with commitment and discipline, and you can achieve it. We need to continually challenge ourselves and expect more out of life. Take up a new sport, learn a language, move to a new location, change your career, or get involved with voluntary work and give back to others. Setting objectives and following through helps us obtain them. By visualizing the outcome daily, you get closer to reaching it. As you progress, you learn; as you learn, you grow; as you grow, you excel.

Make sure you continue with your intentions, for there is strength in purpose and power in consistency. Certainty is one of the greatest human traits we have—an invincible conviction and belief that moves us forward. If your goals take longer, learn to readjust and continually follow through; grow with the process. Frank Lloyd Wright wrote, "*I know the price of success: dedication, hard work, and an unremitting devotion to the things you want to see happen.*" Never deviate from your potential or belief; trust your instinct and vision even if, at times, you get lost in it. Once you have completed one level, continue to the next and improve on it. Build on your momentum. Just never limit yourself, find excuses or allow others to dictate your future or capability. Malcolm Forbes wrote, "*When you cease to dream you cease to live.*" You really can do anything you want, but you must see it and believe in it. Remember that whatever you put into something is usually what you get out of it—what you value and spend time on will be rewarded. There is a real force behind confidence and persistence. Your potential is infinite; we are the ones who set the limits. Believe in what you can do and set out to accomplish it.

I remember hearing the following story many years ago and it has never left my mind. It is about having a great dream, setting an impossible goal, and then realizing it. You see, accomplishment or excellence is more than just powerful thinking or positive thoughts, but it is the elixir that facilitates the results. Commitment, dedication, and hard work are the key attributes to success, but you have to have the vision first.

## *The Power of Vision*

In 1936, the first African American track star Jesse Owens came back from the Berlin Olympics a winner, with four gold medals against all odds. He stunned Germany and astounded the world. No one expected such a success, but he had achieved it. As he arrived at the airport, there was a large press conference held for him. One of the reporters asked, "*Jesse, how did you do it? How did you beat Hitler in his own home town?*" Jesse was quick to answer and said, "*It all started many years ago when I was in junior high school and the coach gave us a speech I never forgot. He said, 'Boys, you can do anything you put your mind to do.'*" Immediately after saying that, Jesse replied, "*Coach, I know what I want to be. I want to be the fastest man in the world.*" The coach answered, "*Well Jesse, that's quite a dream; in fact, it's probably one of the biggest dreams I have ever heard. And Jesse, there's just one problem with that."* Jesse asked, *"What's that coach?"* The Coach gave Jessie the key to success that carried him through the rest of his life. He said, *"Dreams are like clouds, they kind of float around up there, and they can never become accomplished until you build a ladder that will help you climb up, and make those dreams become a reality."*

## *Touching Your Potential*

### Key Concepts and Focus

- You have not even touched your potential.
- Everyone has unique talents waiting to be discovered and utilized.
- Never deviate from your goals or what you truly want out of life.
- Create a powerful plan for your future and continually work toward it.
- Share your plans with someone special, form accountability, and build an alliance.

# 4

## *Attitude Is Everything*

*"Life is either a daring adventure*
*or nothing."* – Helen Keller

In life, attitude is everything. What we believe and how we perceive things will determine our future. Our behavior and focus will dictate the outcome of our day and what we achieve in a lifetime. Charles Swindoll wrote, *"I am convinced that life is 10% what happens to me and 90% how I react to it."* Our perception and how we react to people, difficulties, and problems is crucial to success and achieving our desired outcome. Attitude drives behavior that drives the direction of our lives. If we want things to change positively on the outside, we must first change on the inside. William James wrote, *"The greatest revolution of our generation is the discovery that human beings, by changing the inner attitudes of their minds, can change the outer aspects of their lives."* Obstacles can distract us, and frustration leads only to defeat. Instead of being the victim of events, we can literally dictate to them. Regardless of circumstances, never fall into the trap of getting angry or losing site of what is important.

There is nothing more exhilarating than meeting someone with an attitude to win. Whether it is in sports or business, those who succeed believe they can. They never measure life by every single defeat or immediate setback. They simply focus on the end result and work at achieving it. Vince Lombardi wrote, "*The price of success is hard work, dedication to the job at hand, and the determination that whether we win or lose, we have applied the best of ourselves to the task at hand.*" If you want to drive yourself forward successfully, you must form a daily routine of staying focused and motivated on your objectives. By simply having a constructive outlook, you immediately increase your potential to accomplish more. It remains up to us how we approach everything in our lives: career, relationships, and family. Regardless of past experiences, we can change our behavior and outlook in a minute. Attitude dictates results.

> *Your living is determined not so much by what life brings to you as by the attitude you bring to life; not so much by what happens to you as by the way your mind looks at what happens. Circumstances and situations do color life, but you have been given the mind to choose what the color shall be.* – John Homer Miller

An attitude is simply a learned behavior in responding to people or situations, something we have trained our mind to think. Negative patterns can be broken, however, and destructive assumptions can be realigned to positive associations. Research on behavioral and cognitive science shows that those with positive attitudes can achieve more in a day, live longer, and obtain more successful lives than those without it. The brain sometimes works against us, so we need to reprogram it. Our attitude, whether positive or negative, will strongly influence the outcome in any situation. Nothing dictates how we must feel or react. If we feel angry or discouraged about something, that is our decision. But, if we remain calm and look for a solution, we can solve it. The reaction is up to the individual. When upsetting or discouraging thoughts enter your mind, learn to replace them quickly with encouraging ones. Adapt new associations with old beliefs. Augustus William Hare wrote, *"What is possible? What you will."* Since we have a choice, it is far more productive to react constructively rather than negatively. Whatever event or difficulty you encounter, be proactive not reactive.

Despite the problem, your response will determine the outcome. If an incident bothers you, get your mind off it, at least for twenty minutes. Walk away and catch your breath. Sometimes, give it a day and wait for tomorrow. This gives you time to compose yourself and collect your thoughts. Never immediately act with anger or allow yourself to get discouraged. Ninety-nine percent of the time, you will regret it. Marcus Aurelius Antoninus wrote, *"Consider how much more you often suffer from your anger and grief, than from those very things for which you are angry and grieved."* If something goes wrong, remain composed and quick to solve it. When upset, learn to work through it and move forward. A determined and positive attitude will set into motion the power you need to accomplish anything you want. This type of approach adds more success to your day and excitement to your life. But, it takes discipline and conditioning. Although some habits are hard to break, work at forming a new mental routine. Raise yourself above the circumstances; rehearse encouraging thoughts; continually focus on the outcome of your goals; attack negativity with something productive; and never allow your mind to waiver from what you want.

People who live with passion and connect to a larger vision than themselves create a purpose that pulls them forward. If you believe something is impossible, you are right; but if you believe anything is achievable, then you have started on the path to accomplish it. Know that your determination and attitude is stronger than anything that can happen to you. Certainty and drive are invincible allies. Nothing is more intoxicating or inspiring than those who can stand firm and confident when the world seems to move against them. You see, events come and go, and they will go. Those who remain strong and work through them gain victory and success. Andrew Carnegie wrote, *"If you want to be happy, set a goal that commands your thoughts, liberates your energy, and inspires your hope."* Developing a proactive attitude may take time and discipline, but the outcome is extraordinary. The more we practice, the stronger we become. Eddie Robinson wrote, *"The will to win, the desire to succeed, the urge to reach your full potential . . . these are the keys that will unlock the door to personal excellence."* Attitude is an essential principle in life that will drive us forward and dictate events. There is power in perception; the vision to see what is possible and achieve what is incredible.

I first read about King Gillette, the innovator of the disposable razor, in the book *Will and Vision*. The book profiles successful companies and the leaders that founded them. It was fascinating to read about the tremendous setbacks each person went through. Although none of them had any immediate success, they simply formed the attitude to win. They had an extraordinary vision and determined will to accomplish their goals. Stories and examples are important, because they remind us that we are not alone when it comes to meeting resistance or obstacles. And whatever your ambitions, you can achieve them.

## *Determined to Succeed*

Born in Fond du Lac, Wisconsin in 1855, King Camp Gillette had the mindset to accomplish something great in life. Needing to earn money, he left school early and worked as a traveling salesman. For years, he tried to improve on past inventions or come up with a product that people needed, but nothing ever came of it. By the age of forty, he became discouraged, yet he never gave up and remained determined to succeed. Then the following year in 1895, Gillette started working for Crown Cork & Seal Co, which was responsible for the crown caps on carbonated bottles. Gillette observed that the caps were thrown away after opening the bottle. He realized the value in establishing a business on a disposable product.

As he began to shave for work, he became irritated that his razor was dull and would no longer cut (razor blades needed continuous sharpening and were expensive). Gillette suddenly realized the potential in inventing an inexpensive disposable blade. He established a company and worked for five years trying to perfect it. Gillette finally improved on earlier designs and introduced an innovative high profit-margin stamped steel blade. In 1904, he received a patent for the idea of a double-edged razor and renamed his business the Gillette Safety Razor Company. He soon sold millions of his product and the company eventually became an international phenomenon. It took King Gillette over 17 years to realize his dream, but he remained persistent and developed an attitude to succeed.

## *Attitude Is Everything*

### Key Concepts and Focus

- We are what we think about all day long.
- How we perceive things will determine our future.
- A positive and proactive attitude creates powerful results.
- It is not what others think, but what we believe that drives us forward.
- We can achieve anything we want to if we believe we can.

# 5

# *No More Anchors*

*"Never look back unless you are planning
on going that way."* – Oscar Wilde

One of the most limiting and destructive things we can do to ourselves is measuring our current life by past failures or hardships. We are all prone to mistakes and disappointments. Sometimes they are beyond our control. Many times they just happen, but to hold on to them, to drag them around and allow them to still influence us, is the greatest mistake of all. Keep and treasure your exciting memories and encouraging experiences, but let go of those that discourage or upset you. They weaken and undermine your ability to go forward. Those who look back fall back; those who seek to move on succeed. William Shakespeare wrote, *"Things without remedy, should be without regard; what is done, is done."* Regardless of problems or mistakes, learn from them, and then let go. Yesterday was a decade ago—no more anchors.

Never let the past distort or rob you of your potential. Break the habit of looking back and allowing damaging thoughts to measure your worth or value. Perhaps it was a discouraging comment or painful event. By holding on to it or reviewing it in your mind, you allow it to drag you down. Even if you encountered an upsetting incident yesterday, let it go. What value is there in holding onto it? Every day is a chance to reset and move forward proactively. Seneca wrote, *"While we are postponing, life speeds by."* Spending time remembering hurtful events or past failures simply pulls us back to that moment. Returning to discouraging thoughts is counterproductive. Always remain focused on what is important, such as your goals and objectives. What we believe and how we think daily will determine the course of our future.

Two parts of the brain that deal directly with memory are the Hippocampus, which deals with short term, and the Reticular Activating System, which is the part of the brain centered on motivation. The RAS is like a filter between your conscious mind and your subconscious mind. It takes instructions from your current thoughts and passes them on to your subconscious. It tends to believe whatever messages you give it and will hold on to them as long as you allow it. The more we rehearse something in our mind, the more we program it (this is how memories are formed). If we keep returning and repeating the event, it becomes permanent. But by ignoring unpleasant or discouraging thoughts, we can eliminate them. When a negative thought returns, just push it out and replace it with a thought of something encouraging or exciting. If you remember a past failure, immediately think about what you learned from that experience or how you will achieve success in the future. Focus on the results you want or desire. Learn to direct your thoughts to the things that fulfill your objectives. Shift your mind back to things that offer you encouragement and enthusiasm. This will take time and practice, but it works.

In many cases, misfortunes and failures strengthen and improve us. They are a powerful force that pushes us forward if we embrace them. Never allow these setbacks to hinder or restrain you. Learn from them, and move on to the next thing. Domenico Cieri Estrada wrote, "*Bring the past only if you are going to build from it.*" Anyone who has achieved great success has gone through a succession of trials and errors. This is the systematic process of learning. The larger the goals or objectives, the more we gain along the way. James Joyce wrote, "*Mistakes are the portals of discovery.*" Letting go of discouraging thoughts takes discipline and mental strength, but you can achieve incredible results by being proactive. Never waste time on what you cannot fix or a problem you do not control. Always progress forward and leave that history behind where it belongs.

There is often a conflict between who we are and what we want to become; where we have been and where we are going. Focus on the results you want and confidently move in that direction. If you had a bad experience or made a mistake, gather what you can and refocus on where you are going. Euripides wrote, "*There is in the worst of fortune the best of chances for a happy change.*" Never allow these things to weigh you down or pull you back. Holding on to the past weakens the soul and undermines your future. It is a debilitating habit that takes time to break, but you can break it. Negative thoughts are like an anchor restraining you, and keeping you from moving; a weight that makes the journey harder. Think what happens when a ship moves forward, sails full of wind, but the anchor is still down. The force of the pushing and holding eventually rip the boat apart. Learn to raise the anchor. Each time you do, you take another step closer of ridding yourself of that weight entirely.

Compare this to going to a new job or even starting a new relationship, and dragging suitcases filled with problems behind us. We lug these bags around wherever we go, stumbling over them every which way we turn. The longer we hang on to them, the more frustrated we become. No one needs extra baggage or to carry what will not help them. Maybe it was a dead-end job, failed career, destructive friendship, or uncomfortable relationship. Learn to let go. There is a powerful and liberating feeling in releasing these negative memories and moving ahead. Find the freedom and confidence of developing your attitude, and the exhilaration of strength that comes from continuing ahead. James Russell Miller wrote, "*If you will call your troubles experiences and remember that every experience develops some latent force within you, you will grow vigorous and happy however adverse your circumstances may seem to be.*" So regardless of what happened, grow forward; take what you can and learn what not to do in the future. Remember, yesterday was a decade ago. No more anchors.

One of the most powerful poems ever written is Rudyard Kipling's *If*. It seems to personify an incredible and powerful ideal of how to live; a balance between reality and how we choose to confront it. The poem offers the choices we can make, the strength we can gather, and the decision to always move ahead. The poem was actually based on Sir Leander Starr Jameson, a friend Kipling met in South Africa in 1897. Jameson was trying to help organize the colonies and was involved in a disastrous military raid that ended in failure. Jameson was made a scapegoat and faced terrible consequences afterwards. Yet he somehow pulled himself together and moved forward with dignity and honor. The poem celebrates the courage and character Jameson embodied, even after he was wrongfully blamed.

# *If*

*If you can keep your head when all about you*
*Are losing theirs and blaming it on you;*
*If you can trust yourself when all men doubt you,*
*But make allowance for their doubting too;*
*If you can wait and not be tired by waiting,*
*Or being lied about, don't deal in lies,*
*Or, being hated, don't give way to hating,*
*And yet don't look too good, nor talk too wise;*

*If you can dream—and not make dreams your master,*
*If can think, and not make your thoughts your aim;*
*If you can meet with triumph and disaster*
*And treat both those impostors just the same;*
*If you can bear to hear the truth you've spoken*
*Twisted by knaves to make a trap for fools,*
*Or watch the things you gave your life to, broken,*
*And stoop and build'em up with worn out tools;*

*If you can make one heap of all your winnings*
*And risk it on one turn of pitch-and-toss,*
*And lose, and start again at your beginnings*
*And never breathe a word about your loss;*
*If you can force your heart and nerve and sinew*
*To serve your turn long after they are gone,*
*And so hold on when there is nothing in you*
*Except the Will which says to them: "Hold on";*

*If you can talk with crowds and keep your virtue,*
*Or walk with kings—nor lose the common touch;*
*If neither foe nor loving friends can hurt you;*
*If all men count with you, but none too much;*
*If you can fill the unforgiving minute*
*With sixty seconds' worth of distance run—*
*Yours is the Earth and everything that's in it,*
*And—which is more—you'll be a Man, my son!*
- Rudyard Kipling

# *No More Anchors*

## Key Concepts and Focus

- Yesterday was a decade ago.  No more anchors.
- If we do not learn from our past, we are destined to repeat it.
- Remember negative thoughts undermine our life.
- Never allow the past to rob you of your present.
- Regardless of what has happened, gather what you can and move forward.
- Whenever the past returns, be quick to put it in its place, and think about what you are going to accomplish in the future.

# Strength

**6** *The Art of Discipline*

**7** *Attack Your Weak Points*

**8** *Failure is Not an Option*

**9** *Dictate to Events*

**10** *No Excuses, Only Solutions*

# 6

## *The Art of Discipline*

*"Nothing worthwhile ever happens quickly
and easily. You achieve only as you are
determined to achieve."* – Robert H. Lauer

Setting goals and objectives are powerful ways to guide your life to a successful outcome, but just writing them down or focusing on them is not enough. We need to put action behind our plans continually; something that is pursued daily. Just as great athletes practice every day to improve their performance, we need to set a specific criterion to accomplish what we want out of life. It is our dedication and commitment that creates the momentum for achievement. Build on today by outperforming yesterday. The Webster dictionary defines discipline as: *"training that corrects, molds, or perfects the mental faculties or moral character."* It is a balance between the physical activity of preparation and the mental improvement of the mind—a continued practice of development, learning, and perfection. While the thinking and planning of an objective is significant, the daily rituals of activities and consistency are critical. Jim Rohn wrote, *"Discipline is the bridge between goals and accomplishments."* Your continual diligence and endurance are powerful catalysts that produce lasting results.

Anything worth doing well takes practice and dedication. Learn to form positive habits and schedule the time each day to work toward your goals. By setting up a daily routine of objectives, whether working out to increase our physical condition or personal goals in business and life, we must always commit the proper time and focus. Discipline is about following through, even when we are not in the mood or feel like doing something. While it is easy to get distracted or procrastinate, excuses lead only to failure. Action is the difference between excellence and mediocrity—always doing your best or settling for less. Henry Ward Beecher wrote, *"Hold yourself responsible for a higher standard than anybody else expects of you. Never excuse yourself."* Any great accomplishment in life represents dedicated hours of discipline and dedication.

Whether advancing in a sport, progressing in a career, or truly reaching your potential, it starts with discipline. Tremendous athletes are just that because they spend the extra time training. They are dedicated professionals who set up a specific schedule of activities and continually follow through. They constantly perfect the basics and build on their talent. Often, it is not about feeling motivated 90% of the time, but continuing through the 10% when feeling tired or unmotivated. These are the moments we need to push ourselves and do what is necessary. Ray A. Kroc wrote, *"Press on. Nothing in the world can take the place of persistence."* Anything is possible with continued commitment and effort. Form the mental attitude that no matter what happens, you accomplish your daily objectives. Focus on the end result you are trying to achieve and the success you hope to accomplish. Remember why you are doing it; the reason behind your goal. This provides enthusiasm and facilitates the process. It creates the motivation you need and strength to continue.

Sometimes the first step is the hardest. Perhaps it is losing weight, looking for a new job, getting involved in an activity, or going back to school, but take that initiative. You have to make that phone call, rewrite the resume, or fill out the applications.

A Chinese proverb states, "*A journey of the thousand miles begins with a single step.*" Make that stride, for each movement soon becomes a mile and leads you further along the path you desire. You can build on this progress, but it takes self-control and consistency. The greater the goals, the more time you will need. Take advantage of the day, and seize the moment. Never make excuses, and always accomplish what you have scheduled to do. Arnold Bennett wrote, "*We shall never have more time. We have, and have always had, all the time there is. No object is served in waiting until next week or even until tomorrow... Having decided to achieve a task, achieve it at all costs.*" Determination and focus moves us forward and produces powerful results. Anything in this world is possible; a goal, an achievement, even a miracle, but we need discipline to accomplish it.

The following story is one of the greatest moments in sports history. It represents what can happen even when setting an inconceivable goal—something that would appear impossible by all logical observations. While it takes someone with vision to set such an ambition, it also takes an enormous amount of effort, energy, and discipline.

## *The Miracle*

During the 1980 Olympics, the USSR's hockey team was considered number one in the world. After their crushing victory in the 1979 World Championship, the Soviets seemed invincible. Although the Americans were underdogs, they were competitive. Their hopes and abilities were formed by their coach, Herb Brooks. Known for his stubborn personality and fanatical preparation, he understood what it takes to win. After spending a year-and-a-half developing his team, he still continually pushed them. There was no matching the Europeans in skill, so Brooks emphasized speed, conditioning and above all, discipline. The players started practice early in the morning and worked late into the night. They never trained so hard or skated so much, but Brooks worked to unite them, challenging them mentally and physically.

When they played a pre-Olympic exhibition game against the Soviets, the Americans were trampled 10-3; a painful and devastating defeat. Yet the team stayed focused. When the official Olympics began, they went on to beat Sweden, Czechoslovakia and Germany before they once again faced off against the Soviets. The U.S. team fell behind early in the first period, but was able to tie the score 2-2 by the first half. As the second half started, the Soviets took the lead, but the U.S quickly tied again with 3-3. In the last quarter, with only ten minutes left, the U.S. scored the final goal. What is considered one of the greatest moments in sports history, the Americans won a 4-3 upset against the Soviets; this victory lead them on to an Olympic Gold medal. Sports Illustrated wrote, *"It may just be the single most indelible moment in all of U.S. sports history. One that sent an entire nation into a frenzy."* Brooks' continued focus, pushing each player to excel and building on their strengths produced a powerful, disciplined and successful team.

## *The Art of Discipline*

### Key Concepts and Focus

- Continued discipline is the catalyst behind achievement and success.
- We need to put action behind our plans continually.
- Take the initiative today and stay with goal until it is completed.
- Never get distracted or make excuses—just follow through.
- Our established routine becomes easier with time and focus.

# 7

## *Attack Your Weak Points*

*"The only conquests which are permanent
and leave no regrets are our conquests over
ourselves."* – Napoleon Bonaparte

No time in life should be spent discouraged or feeling less than
we are. Certain things that cause us irritation or annoyance,
consciously and subconsciously, hold back our progress. We all
have areas in our life that could be considered inadequate or
ineffective. They make us feel uncomfortable or disconnected
with our surroundings. Whether skills or attributes, they can
cause unnecessary frustration and hinder us from reaching
our true potential. Although no one is great at everything, and
some have more refined talents or abilities, learn to attack your
weak areas and turn them into strengths. Disciplined approach
will help you overcome these deficiencies and become more
proficient and well balanced. Helen Keller wrote, *"We can do
anything we want to do if we stick to it long enough."* Begin what
you want to improve and stay with it until it is completed. What
can be accomplished with just one hour a day over a few months
of time is amazing.

This does not mean that we need to master everything or
become an expert in every area, but we alone have the choice to

expand and further our ability—to turn frustration or insecurity into power and enthusiasm. William Faulkner wrote, "*Do not bother just to be better than your contemporaries or predecessors. Try to be better than yourself.*" There is no limit to what the human mind can accomplish if you are committed and dedicated to improving. Never make excuses or downplay these flaws; simply improve them. Make them a priority and turn them into your strong points. Instead of being intimidated by what you never learned or do not know, attack these areas and become proficient in them. Continually dwelling on our deficiencies bogs us down and prevents us from moving forward. For example, if effectively communicating with others has never been your strength, take a public speaking class. Think of what could be accomplished in life and business by feeling more confident in front of a crowd or in talking with clients. Conquering this skill alone could advance your life and career emotionally and financially.

> **Communication:** The quality of our life is measured by the quality of our communication. What we say and how we communicate it can ascertain if we will succeed or fail. This fundamental proficiency is essential in careers and relationships; yet, over ninety percent of the population fails to convey their thoughts and needs properly or consistently either in a social or business environment. We live in a society of quick hellos and fast memos, but rarely engage in genuine conversations. Our comments are superficial, lacking in creditability, and are more flash than substance. And we wonder why friendships waiver, companies falter, and relationships break down? How can we expect others to understand our needs if we are not encouraging an exchange of ideas?

Reflecting on your past, you will realize how many problems were caused by poor communication: what you should have conveyed, what could have been clearer, or what was never said, causing plans to fail, businesses to suffer, and relationships to dissolve. One of the main reasons why seemingly good marriages end prematurely is the failure to communicate. Neither person lets the other know what is expected, needed, or cared about. If you want to improve the quality of your life, convey your thoughts and messages clearly and consistently. Work on improving your communication skills with your friends, children, family and business associates. Never assume anything. Learn to ask questions, and listen to the answers intently to demonstrate your sincere interest. Be clear and specific. In business meetings, write a list of everything you want to cover; in friendships, let others know your thoughts; and in relationships, build a foundation on clear communication and expectations.

What you discover along the way can be truly extraordinary: people you meet, talent you uncover, and dormant skills waiting to flourish. Socrates wrote, *"The unexamined life is not worth living."* One never knows what exciting skills could be discovered or revealed during the process of development. Attack the areas you want to advance in, such as writing, technology, parenting, or relationships. Research the Internet, find the right books, take a class, and/or talk to an expert. Look into college courses or special programs offered at work or a library. A myriad of opportunities and resources are available. Learn new skills and discover the freedom of conquering these areas in your life. C. W. Barrow wrote, *"Everything can be improved."* Most important is finding the time to improve your life. Procrastination is your downfall. Only the excuses we keep telling ourselves keep us from advancing. Start on a quest to enhance your skills and abilities today. Strengthen your weaknesses, and find the resolve to improve your life. We can do or improve anything we put our mind to. It just takes time and dedication.

One of the most extraordinary stories I ever read was about Helen Keller. Even to this day, her determination and accomplishments are remarkable. It is almost impossible to imagine overcoming such difficulties. In the face of what she overcame, I find it hard to make excuses why I could not accomplish something or try just a bit harder. It proves that any deficiency can be conquered and turned into something very powerful.

## *Out of Darkness*

Helen Keller was born in 1880 in the rural outskirts of Tuscumbia, Alabama. When she was only nineteen months old, she contracted an illness that left her deaf and blind. By age seven, she learned 60 home signs (a type of sign language) to communicate with her family, but there was little hope for any future progress. Her mother Kate, was determined to help her daughter and eventually contacted the Perkins Institute for the Blind in Boston, Massachusetts. The school recommended a teacher by the name of Ann Sullivan, who herself had overcome partial blindness and a difficult childhood. This began a profound relationship between the two that lasted 49 years. With little ability to communicate, Helen was a difficult student; but Sullivan was a dedicated teacher who refused to give up.

She broke through the isolation by using objects to communicate and taught Helen how to fingerspell, write, and read Brail. With her continued commitment and desire for knowledge, Helen attended Radcliff College in 1900 and graduated magna cum laude. She advanced in her studies, learning how to read English, French, German, Greek, and Latin in Braille. Helen eventually became an advocate for people with disabilities and other causes. She learned to speak and traveled with Sullivan to 39 countries, becoming a world-renowned lecturer and author. She wrote numerous articles and published twelve books in her lifetime. In 1915, she founded the Helen Keller International Organization, devoted to research in vision, health, and nutrition. Among her many awards, Helen received the Presidential Medal of Freedom. Helen Keller was a woman who never let her deficiencies or disabilities stand in her way. Through commitment and discipline, she turned her weaknesses into strengths.

# *Attack Your Weak Points*

### Key Concepts and Focus
- Attack your weak points and make them your strong points.
- Only the excuses we tell ourselves impede our ability to improve.
- There is no limit to what we can accomplish if we are determined.
- Pick something you want to improve or enhance and start today.
- Spend a few hours a week on this subject and stay with it.
- Within one month, you will be amazed at how much progress you have made.

# 8

## *Failure Is Not an Option*

*"Never confuse a single defeat with a
final defeat."* – F. Scott Fitzgerald

Much has been written about failure, how it is measured, and
what it means. The correct definition, however, is how you
perceive it. If we move forward with confidence and purpose
toward a target or goal, we will eventually hit it. We may go
through many trials or years of setbacks, but in the end we can
achieve our objective if we never give up. Only when we let go of
a dream or goal do we really lose what we could have had. Elbert
Hubbard wrote, *"There is no failure except in no longer trying."*
However, ambition often involves risks: the risk of uncertainty;
the unknown; the undiscovered; what we may lose; but what we
may learn and gain makes that all worthwhile. If we truly wish
to succeed, we must conquer these fears, accept that we will
make mistakes, and endure setbacks. Remain focused on what
you want and be flexible when things go wrong. Frank Tyger
wrote, *"To be successful, you've got to be willing to fail."* History
is not filled with triumphant stories of those that had an easy
journey from start to finish. Everyone goes through setbacks
and defeats, but those who are determined to win get up and

keep going. Confucius wrote, *"Our greatest glory is not in ever falling, but in rising every time we fall."*

Making lists and scheduling time for our goals is the first step toward achieving them. They create a framework for our ambitions and put drive behind are actions; but putting a specific time limit on a goal or ambition can be tricky. In some cases, when the time has elapsed and the goal is not achieved, we lose hope or become overwhelmingly discouraged. This is one of the worst things that can happen to the human spirit. It can be crushing and debilitating. Countless thousands gave up as they stood only inches away from total victory. Never allow that to happen to you. Do not give up on yourself or become complacent. Sometimes we have the right goal, just not the right timing. And timing is everything.

> *Let's learn and label properly Disappointment and Discouragement for what they are—two completely different states of mind. Disappointment can be a spur to improvement that will contribute to success. But Discouragement is a mortal enemy that destroys courage and robs one of the will to fight. It is not circumstance that cause Discouragement, but one's own reaction to that circumstance. Everyone must meet Disappointment, many times; it is simply a part of life. When it is met, we may resign ourselves to Discouragement and failure. Or we may recognize each Disappointment as an asset by which we can profit, and take new strength from a lesson learned. The choice is ours, each time, to make.* – John M. Wilson

What facilitates achievement and success is attitude—to believe you can, regardless of how long it takes. Learn to keep going, for drive and persistence will eventually overcome any obstacles. The global company Federal Express was merely a concept and ignored by most as being impossible. On a business plan prepared for his college Economics class at Yale, the founder, Fred Smith, received a C (the professor thought the idea was ridiculous). Yet Smith still believed the concept of a private global mail services could work. After years of planning and preparation, the company's first attempt was a disaster. Only seven of the 130 packages sent got there on time! But Smith never gave up and kept improving on his idea. He took the past problems and turned them into solutions. He refined his business model and figured out how to make the company succeed. It took years of dedication and persistence, but FedEx is now a multi-billion dollar international enterprise. He stated, *"Fear of failure must never be a reason not to try something."*

During the American Revolution, the General Nathanial Green, fighting the British in the Southern colonies, lost 13 of his 17 engagements with the enemy. However, he kept fighting and stayed focused on the larger objective: winning the war, not just a battle. His determination and consistency wore down the enemy and caused them to lose hope. They became frustrated and discouraged. After years of conflict, the British finally pulled out many of their forces from the southern colonies. Nathanial eventually won the war in the South, which contributed to American's victory and independence. In fact, so many great achievers failed more than they succeeded, but it was in these few successes that they left their legacy. Part of their contribution to achievement was the attitude of never giving up—staying with something until realized, regardless of how long it took. Dennis Mahoney wrote, *"Lack of will power and drive cause more failure than lack of imagination and ability."*

When choosing an objective, create the purpose and confidence to achieve it. Put passion and commitment behind it. By setting our mind on a goal, we unlock a great force inside us. When we believe we can succeed, there is nothing in life that can stop us except ourselves. Just continue forward and keep your sight on the end objective. Robert Schuller wrote, *"Failure doesn't mean you are a failure . . . it just means you haven't succeeded yet."* In anything you do, have the mindset that failure is not an option. Never allow anyone to tell you what you can or cannot do. Never find yourself limiting your goals because of past setbacks or perceived ability. Anything is possible if you believe it: a new job, home, business, marriage, or family. You may not always obtain what you desire immediately, but the difference is that you stay with it and never settle for less. It is great to create a plan and timeframe, but remain persistent and flexible. Through the course of achieving our ambitions, we learn from our mistakes, refine our objectives, and grow stronger during the process.

> *Don't be discouraged by a failure. It can be a positive experience. Failure is, in a sense, the highway to success, inasmuch as every discovery of what is false leads us to seek earnestly after what is true, and every fresh experience points out some form of error which we shall afterwards carefully avoid.* – John Keats

Learn to form a mental capacity for success—a positive outlook with the expectation of accomplishing your goals. We stand a far better chance at hitting our target if we aim for it, so aim high. If you go into a game with the intention of winning and believe you can, the odds are increased considerably, regardless of the competition. Be willing to continue on until you have accomplished what you wanted and obtained victory. With this outlook, failure is not an option. Any impediment is quickly managed, then disregarded. During the process, you develop your character and refine your skills. Adversity tests only our resolve and strengthens our purpose. By visualizing what you want, you eventually align your intentions with the outcome and obtain it. Remember, the word *failure* belongs only in the dictionary of fools.

I was in a research room years ago dedicated to a remarkable man. The shelves were filled with hundreds of books written about his life and accomplishments. Then hanging on the wall I spotted a simple frame with a paragraph inside it. The title read *Failure,* and continued on with the description of his life.

# *Failure*

Growing up in a poverty stricken home, he received no formal education or hope for a successful future. His beloved mother died when he was only nine years old, leaving him with an uncaring father. Ambitious, yet uneducated, he ran for the legislature in Illinois and was badly beaten. He entered business, failed, and spent the next seventeen years paying up the debts of a worthless partner. He fell in love with a beautiful young woman to whom he became engaged. She then became ill and suddenly died. Heartbroken, he turned to education and taught himself the law on his own. He ran for Congress, yet was overwhelmingly beaten. Next, he tried to get an appointment to the United States Land Office, but was unsuccessful. He eventually became a candidate for the U.S. Senate and was again badly defeated. Staying with politics, he was chosen as a nominee for the vice presidency, but was once more defeated. In the face of all these setbacks and failures, he still never quit trying. His calm fortitude and persistence eventually lead him to achieve one of the highest successes in life, and in 1860, Abraham Lincoln became the thirteenth president of the United States. His strong leadership and steadfast determination lead America through its greatest internal crisis. Lincoln helped win the Civil War and kept the country united. He also introduced measures that resulted in the abolition of slavery, issuing his Emancipation Proclamation, and promoting the passage of the Thirteenth Amendment to the Constitution. Today, many scholars deem him as the greatest president the United States ever had. For Abraham Lincoln, failure was never an option.

# Failure Is Not an Option

## Key Concepts and Focus

- Failure is not an actuality; it is a perception.
- How we perceive defeats will determine our future.
- Learn from mistakes and build on them.
- Always remain focused on what you want, not the obstacles or setbacks along the way.
- Avoid discouragement, and replace it with determination.
- Anything is possible if you simply believe it is.

# 9

## *Dictate to Events*

*"Either I will find a way, or I will make one."*
–Sir Walter Sidney

Too often we take a defensive attitude when events or calamities arise. We act surprised, get frustrated, or just give up. These obstacles or defeats can have a profound effect on our hopes and future. They immediately divert our attention and slow our momentum. We become the victim, weakening our mentality and our ability to drive forward. By allowing these negative distractions to dictate to us, they can guide our thoughts and distract us from the results we want. Yet hitting an impediment is common. In fact, it should be expected when striving toward your ambitions. The road is seldom straight, and there will be speed bumps. Frank A. Clark wrote, *"If you find a path with no obstacles, it probably doesn't lead anywhere."* The longer our journey, and the more we desire out of life, the higher the barriers. Be prepared for them, but do not get distracted by them.

When trying to advance, change, or grow, we will always meet some form of resistance. Often the larger the objective, the more difficulties occur. It is how we interpret these problems—our attitude—that will bring success in achieving our objectives.

Hannah Moore wrote, "*Obstacles are those frightful things you see when you take your eyes off the goal.*" Never get sidetracked because you hit a wall. Go around it or over it, but never let an event dictate to you if it is not the result you want. If you are certain of what you want and believe in your objective, then stay with it. Persistence can often be revealing and exhilarating. While searching for a yes, never settle for a no; never deviate from your purpose.

If you cannot find a way, make one. If there is no opportunity, create it. Be perceptive, inventive, and find another way. Moliere wrote, "*The greater the obstacle the more glory in overcoming it.*" We often approach things conventionally when we should be thinking outside the box—attacking problems from another angle. Instead of thinking lineally and hitting things directly on, sometimes we need to out flank it and try something different. There are extraordinary opportunities around us every day. We just need to look for them and recognize them. Spend some time alone walking through options; get away for a weekend and refresh your mind; brainstorm with a colleague or friend; form an alliance or group to help you. Allow yourself to be creative and imaginative. You may discover a side of you that had always remained hidden. If everything was easy, we would tend to not appreciate the results. Enjoy the ride and prove to yourself what you are made of: your character, discipline, and resolve.

> *You can surmount the obstacles in your path if you are determined, courageous and hard-working. Never be fainthearted. Be resolute, but never bitter. Bitterness will serve only to warp your personality. Permit no one to dissuade you from pursuing the goals you set for yourself. Do not fear to pioneer, to venture down new paths of endeavor.* – Ralph J. Bunche

You may be applying for a new position or job, but seem to get nowhere. Perhaps it is time to review your resume, have someone else critique it, redesign it, or create another one. Perhaps the direction you have chosen is not really what you want to do. It might seem safe or something you know well, but it is not your passion or what is really inside you. How often we settle for less than what we are, because we think it needs to be that way. We all have incredible gifts. Use them. Know what you are worth and get it. Try something new, discover other skills, or research an industry you have always been fascinated with. You may meet interesting people, form new friendships, or find the perfect career that seemed impossible. So much can be accomplished in just one day if we break out of the self-imposed monotony. Focus on the results you want and the long-term goals, not just what happens every minute or hour of the day. See the end, and trust in the journey.

Never let people discourage you from accomplishing something special or extraordinary. Never let anyone or anything set limits on your potential. Know what you want out of the situation and continue on until you have realized it. By creating the strength and endurance you need, obstacles will no longer influence you; the stronger your resolve, the faster the outcome. Events will challenge you, but embrace them. Quickly look for a solution or another alternative. Learn to grow and adapt swiftly. Harlow H. Curtice wrote, "*Let no one or anything stand between you and the difficult task, let nothing deny you this rich chance to gain strength by adversity, confidence by mastery, and success by deserving it . . . Do it better than anyone else can do it.*" By having confidence in yourself and staying focused on your objectives, they will be achieved. To ever settle for less is a compromise, but to continue until you have succeeded is a triumph. Life sometimes brings us up to that last minute, testing our resolve and strength. Often the more conflict we encounter, the closer we are to victory. It is in every difficulty that we are challenged yet strengthened. Problems will test our determination and endurance; but dictate to them, never allow them to dictate to you.

I heard this inspiring story two decades ago. It offered a profound insight into what could be done in even the worst of circumstances. Through this event, Roy has left a legacy for others to follow. I have also read other similar stories about people who received dire information, but decided to do something about it. They ignored defeat and created the capacity within themselves to conquer their fears and live the life they were meant to. It proves that anything is possible.

# *M. T. C.*

His name was Roy Kelly, and in the prime of his life, he was informed that he had terminal cancer. Devastated by the news, he and his wife went home to cry and then prepare to die. Should they keep it a secret from their friends? Well, they thought about it. After awhile of contemplating the news, they felt they should no longer prepare for it, but rather do something about it. So they decided to put on a big party and invited all of their friends. During the festivities, Roy held up his hand to make an announcement. He said, *"You're probably wondering why I've called all of you together here tonight. This is a cancer party! You see, I have been told that I have terminal cancer. But my wife and I realized that we are all terminal. So we decided to start a new organization. It's called: M. T. C.—**Make Today Count**. As of tonight, all of you have become charter members."* The story goes on to say that since then, Roy's organization has grown across the country, reaching thousands of people, and Roy has been too busy to die.

# *Dictate to Events*

### Key Concepts and Focus

- Always dictate to events; never let the events dictate to you.
- In every negative circumstance, there is a positive solution.
- Never let anyone or anything set limits on your potential.
- Often the more conflict we encounter, the closer we are to victory.
- Find the opportunity in everything that happens.

# 10

# *No Excuses, Only Solutions*

*"Many of life's failures are people who did not realize how close they were to success when they gave up." –* Thomas Edison

We should never get caught up in making excuses why something was not done, blame others, or justify our lack of response. As difficulties or impediments arise, it is easy to get trapped into a negative mentality. We often put off problems or issues, allowing them to linger. We procrastinate or become defensive. Yet immediate and direct action is the best solution. Feeling overwhelmed or dealing with setbacks is common enough, but this takes away from our momentum. Donald Marquis wrote, *"Procrastination is the art of keeping up with yesterday."* When we form a positive and proactive approach, one that attacks problems instead of becoming a victim, we move forward more swiftly, increase our resolve, and improve the situation. Nothing is ever gained by making excuses or putting things off. We must act confidently and do what is necessary.

Excuses tend to compromise life and keep us from accomplishing our true potential. Although problems will always occur, this is a good thing; for in each one there is a solution and a chance to learn, an area of discovery, and a challenge to grow.

Norman Vincent Peale wrote, "*Believe it is possible to solve your problem. Tremendous things happen to the believer.*" As we solve small problems, larger ones will surface. This is the nature of life, but once we have formed the attitude of no excuses, only solutions, we are ready and quick to deal with them—never losing time feeling frustrated. We simply attack them, use them to our advantage, learn from the moment, and move on. This positive focus programs our mind as a problem solver; a person who can deal with issues swiftly. It is a skill that people admire and an ability that creates great leaders—a powerful attribute to execute and master. Excuses are why others have failed—they hesitate to act and only add to the difficulties. They have to jump back to deal with an issue instead of focusing on the future and moving forward.

Sometimes the solutions may not be the right ones, but by acting swiftly you have time to adjust and try something different. Frank Tyger wrote, "*The most important thing to do in solving a problem is to begin.*" When proactive, you expand your thoughts, perceiving things on many levels, and find multiple options. If you are unhappy at work, start to look for a new career. Perhaps you want to start your own business or develop a product you invented. Maybe you have a great idea for a novel or book, but just keep putting it off. Sit down, form an outline, and start writing. If you want to be in better shape, get up earlier and start running, or go to a gym after work. Find a good trainer and work with a nutritionist. The only way to make any of these things happen is to do them. Spend time thinking about it, put together a plan, get others involved, find a friend to share the experience, and get to work. We must stop making excuses and begin to solve the problem by not being the problem.

While some difficulties may be large or complicated, the same formula applies. Learn to solve them and work through them. Find an advantage in each one, learn to grow, and never deviate from your objective. Perhaps a benefit learned is what not to do in the future, or you discover a different approach.

Think creatively and pull on resources you never knew you had. Just never put things off, for the best solution is direct action. Harvey S. Firestone wrote, *"You get the best out of others when you get the best out of yourself."* Excuses simply keep us from becoming whom we are. They steal our passion and momentum from life. Whatever the problem, be quick in attacking it, and follow through. Never shrink back in a situation; advance through it.

Edison is a great profile in problem solving. He simply kept going until he figured out how to do something. Every mistake or failure was just a part of the process in solving the problem. He brought in creative minds and knew the importance of working with others to get results. His legacy was built on his persistence and solutions, not excuses.

## *The Power of Persistence*

Thomas Alva Edison was born in 1847 in Ohio. Hearing impaired and considered slow to learn, his teachers thought he was retarded. His mother pulled him out of school and decided to home-school him. By nineteen, Edison was working for Western Union, where he spent time reading and experimenting (he was later fired when the battery acid he used for one of his experiments destroyed his boss' desk). He relocated to New Jersey and continued working long hours trying to figure out how to make something work. Although many inventions took months or even years to perfect, Edison remained focused and committed. He believed in trial-and-error, never giving up looking for another solution to every problem. One of his first breakthroughs came when he succeeded in discovering how to record sound and eventually invented the phonograph. This led to some early recognition and prosperity followed. He expanded his business, hired more employees, and next searched for a way to harness electricity.

Although Edison did not actually invent the light bulb, he was the first to create a commercially practical and lasting product—a bulb that could burn for hundreds and ultimately thousands of hours. It took him over 1000 attempts to find a filament that would last long enough, but he finally discovered the proper solution. With the advancement of his product, he sold the concept to homes and businesses and integrated a system for the distribution of electricity. Edison was a prolific thinker with practical far-reaching ideas and a vision for the future. He applied the principles of mass production and employed teams of inventors to work on his concepts. After another unsuccessful attempt to create a storage battery, he said, "*Well, at least we know 8000 things that don't work.*" Edison eventually established 14 companies, one of them General Electric, and filed 1093 patents for inventions. He is considered one of the most prolific inventors and problem solvers, who once stated, "*I never failed once; it happens to be a 2000 step process.*"

## *No Excuses, Only Solutions*

### Key Concepts and Focus
- Excuses compromise life and keep us from becoming who we are.
- Never make excuses or blame others for difficulties or unsolved problems.
- Always attack problems and find the hidden solutions.
- Seize them and look at it as an opportunity for growth and advancement.
- Whatever the difficulty, be quick in attacking it and follow through.

# *Success*

11  *Moving Forward*

12  *Patient Determination*

13  *Always Learning and Growing*

14  *Flexibility and Adaptability*

15  *Expect Change*

16  *Be Prepared for Success*

# 11

## *Moving Forward*

*"Be ready at any moment to give up what you are
for what you might become."* – W. E. B. Du Bois

We can never go where we need to be when we keep returning
to where we have been. If you have a vision for your life and see
yourself in a certain place or position, then you must move in
that direction with confidence. You must not only be prepared
to grow, but to leave part of your past behind. With anything
new, there is always a sense of apprehension and uncertainty.
What was familiar or even easy in the past is now left behind,
but you must possess the faith and fortitude in your pursuit.
Stay focused on your decision and unwavering along the journey.
You need strong character and resolve to move ahead, letting go
of things that were holding you back. Never allow yourself to
repeat those bad habits or return to those unproductive areas.
Believe in yourself and what must be done, then do it. If we keep
looking back, we will fall back; if we return to where we were,
we cannot advance to where we need to be. William Hazlitt
wrote, *"I like a person who knows his own mind and sticks to it;
who sees at once what, in given circumstances, is to be done, and
does it."* Allow yourself to experience the strength that comes

from your choice, the power in change, and the confidence in moving forward.

Life is our most valuable asset; how we use it creates our own destiny. One essential area of growth is with whom we spend our time. Lincoln wrote, "*A better part of one's life consists of his friendships.*" Although having friends is important, there are some people we would be better off without—those who are discouraging, make us feel uncomfortable, or generally do not share our own ideals. It is great to help others or be there to support them, but if someone is bringing you down or compromising your beliefs, let them go. It may be a hurtful relationship, dishonest associate, bad business partner, or a denigrating friend. Find the courage to move on and surround yourself with the proper environment and individuals. Align yourself with the right group of people: honest but kind, encouraging, understanding, and truly caring. What is a true friend? The dictionary describes friendship as *a relationship which involves mutual respect, esteem, and affection; a person who renders support in the time of need; helping one another and the sharing of a hardship; a person one likes and trusts.* It is better to have three or four great friends you can count on than eight to ten who compromise who you are or make you less than what you can be.

> *Friendship implies loyalty, esteem, cordiality, sympathy, affection, readiness to aid, to help, to stick, to fight for, if need be. The real friend is he or she who can share all our sorrows and double our joys. Radiate friendship and it will return sevenfold.* – B. C. Forbes

The journey forward can be extraordinary, if we allow it. There are so many new things to experience and learn; the joy of accomplishment and the excitement of progress; meeting different people and discovering new places. Yet, it is often tempting to return to idle routines or destructive vices. They sometimes offer comfort or even security, but at the price of progress and improvement. Sometimes it is hard to let go, but trust in the freedom you will feel when you do. In life, growth is everything. We should be learning and advancing daily. With so much future opportunity, it is impossible to move forward if we keep reaching back. We can spend the next decade making excuses or spend today changing our lives. As we aspire to become better and improve, we must learn to let go of what is behind. Emerson wrote, *"Progress is the activity of today."*

Trust in what you have undertaken and never allow the weakness of past failures or bad habits to resurface. Resist destructive temptations and treat mediocrity as sin. Do whatever is necessary to remove what is discouraging and replace it with something productive. Sometimes changing your immediate environment or situation can elevate a moment of weakness. Take a walk, work out, review your goals, read something inspiring, or call an ally. Fortify yourself with supporting friends and productive activities. Smile in the face of adversity and fight the obstacles that hold you back. Let nothing rob you of a chance to improve your life. Henry Theodore Tuckerman wrote, *"Let us recognize the beauty and power of true enthusiasm; and whatever we may do to enlighten ourselves or others, guard against checking or chilling a single earnest sentiment."* You must have the faith in the road you have taken, embrace the things that help you, and enjoy the ride.

This poem is a simple yet powerful example of the decisions we make. Every day we have choices that will dictate certain outcomes. We can go with the flow and settle for less or do something different and discover what we never knew existed.

## *The Road Not Taken*

*Two roads diverged in a yellow wood,*
*And sorry I could not travel both*
*And be one traveler, long I stood*
*And looked down one as far as I could*
*To where it bent in the undergrowth;*

*Then took the other, as just as fair,*
*And having perhaps the better claim,*
*Because it was grassy and wanted wear;*
*Though as for that, the passing there*
*Had worn them really about the same,*

*And both that morning equally lay*
*In leaves no step had trodden black.*
*On, I kept the first for another day!*
*Yet knowing how way leads on to way,*
*I doubt if I should ever come back.*

*I shall be telling this with a sigh*
*Somewhere ages and ages hence:*
*Two roads diverged in a wood, and I—*
*I took the one less traveled by,*
*And that has made all the difference.*
- Robert Frost

## *Moving Forward*

### Key Concepts and Focus

- We can never go where we need to be when we keep returning to where we have been.
- Comfort is often the price of improvement.
- The journey forward can be extraordinary, if we allow it.
- Leave behind what pulls you down and harms your future.

- Trust in your decision for moving forward and have faith in your ability.
- Gain strength in your decision and never be tempted to go back.

# 12

## *Patient Determination*

*"Patience is not passive; on the contrary, it is active; it is concentrated strength."* – Edward G. Bulwer-Lytton

Patience should never be conceived as stillness or a sense of inactivity. It is merely a strong and focused mind set until a goal is achieved or an event realized—a subdued power of concentration and faith that we will obtain something that has not yet come. When you resolve to accomplish an ambition, remain steadfast but persistent. Edwin H. Chapin wrote, *"Impatience never commanded success."* We should always be moving forward with endurance and confidence, for consistency is a necessary attribute of success. Believe you will achieve your ambition and you will. By keeping composed and positive, we never allow time to distract or hinder us from the final outcome. While some objectives may take a few months to finish, others can take years or even decades to complete. But by remaining patient yet determined you set your mind at ease until you have succeeded.

So many unknown events are happening behind the scenes that we need to trust in time. It can be difficult. When we want something, we often seek immediate results or gratification. Sometimes this can happen, but often it takes time for circumstances to align correctly with what we desire. We accomplish nothing by being impatient. By allowing time to control us, we become irritated, frustrated, and eventually discouraged. Soon despair sets in and we give up. When we let go of our goal, we lose; if we hold on, we will eventually have it. John Ruskin wrote, *"It is patience which makes the final difference between those who succeed or fail in all things."* Learn to enjoy the process and get the most out of each day. Always do everything you can and enjoy each hour, but learn the discipline of patience. Balance fortitude with persistence; confidence with certainty.

> *"You can do what you want to do, accomplish what you want to accomplish . . . Not all of a sudden, perhaps, not in one swift and sweeping act of achievement . . . but you can do it gradually—day by day—if you want to do it, if you will to do it, if you work to do it, over a sufficient period of time."*
> – William Holler

Throughout life there are always some things that take time to obtain. Whether it is a job, house, marriage or family, each of these objectives lay in the distance. Patient determination is the calm and grounded attitude to get there. Stacey Charter wrote, *'Life is all about timing: the unreachable becomes reachable, the unattainable becomes attainable, and the unavailable becomes available. Have the patience and wait it out, for it's all about timing."* Enjoy the journey; for a significant element in obtaining the goal is the process in getting there: a reserved quality of appreciation, a powerful maturity of grounded strength, and the assurance in knowing we deserve it. Remain focused on the end result, but have fun along the way. The moments you experience now will add to the quality of the outcome. Becoming discouraged or frustrated accomplishes nothing; but staying focused on what you want will eventually come to fruition. Whatever your goal, patient determination will bring victory and success. Never let time rob you of your confidence or purpose; remain persistent and dedicated. With great challenges come wonderful rewards.

Winston Churchill is an example of someone who was written off long before his time. He was the right man at the right time, but that time was long in coming. However, he remained prepared for that moment, diligent in his pursuits and patient.

## *The Patient Lion*

Sir Winston Leonard Spencer-Churchill was born at Blenheim Palace on November 30, 1874. A descendant from the famous Duke of Marlborough, he was born to a life of influence and privilege. He seemed destined for success. Yet Churchill was a slow learner in school and often punished for his academic failure. His stern father hoped that his son would become a barrister, but Winston did poorly in his studies. Rejected by Oxford and Cambridge, Churchill applied to Royal Military College at Sandhurst, but failed the entrance examination twice. With continual tutoring, he was finally accepted. After graduation, Churchill entered the British Army and became First Lord of the Admiralty. During World War I, however, Churchill helped orchestrate the disastrous Gallipoli Campaign (an attempt to capture Constantinople). Blamed for the failure, Churchill received a demotion. Already discourage and disgraced, he remarked, "*I am finished.*"

After the war, he reentered politics and eventually became Chancellor of the Exchequer in 1924. He petitioned for the return to the Gold Standard, which became an economic catastrophe. This all but ruined his chosen field, and he believed his political career was now over. But he remained patient and determined to succeed. After Germany's loss in World War I, Churchill kept a close eye on that country. In 1932, he continually spoke out against the dangers of

Hitler and his fascist government, but few listened. In 1934, Churchill fought for Britain's need to increase the military, rebuild the Royal Air Force, and create a Ministry of Defense; yet he was often ignored by complacent and passive politicians. After the inevitable outbreak of World War II (September 3, 1939), Churchill was finally appointed First Lord of the Admiralty. With the invasion of Poland, Britain entered the war. By mid 1940, Germany was dominating the continent, capturing Norway, Belgium, and France. With the incumbent Prime Minister Chamberlain's poor leadership and lack of perspective, there was only one man, a born leader, to assume that position, Winston Churchill. His waiting was over.

Now 64, Churchill's determination was stronger than ever. He never compromised with Germany or for any appeasement. He saw the only way to win the war was to defeat Hitler and everything he stood for. Badly outnumbered and ill prepared for Germany's war machine, he used his voice and rhetoric to inspire Britain and motivate its people to victory, saying, "*We shall never surrender.*" Churchill continually struck back at Germany, and his determination frustrated the enemy. He carefully cultivated a relationship with the United States, who entered the war in 1941, and soon built a powerful alliance with the nation. After six long years of fighting, Britain and its alliance went on to win the world's most severe and costly war. It was through his determination and patience that inspired Britain and led it to its greatest victory.

## *Patient Determination*

### Key Concepts and Focus

- Patience is powerful and determination will be rewarded.
- Always remain steadfast but persistent.
- Timing is everything; trust that circumstances are aligning on your behalf.

- Enjoy the journey and experiences along the way. A great deal of obtaining the goal is the process in getting there.
- Always move forward and never give up.

# 13

## *Always Learning and Growing*

*"Learning is like rowing upstream: not to advance is to drop back".* – Chinese Proverb

Realize that in every moment or event is a chance to improve and advance your knowledge. The more information we gather, the more we broaden our mind. Learning is an infinite journey. Yet we should never pretend to know everything or to understand what we do not. All this does is limit us, narrows our options, and destroys an opportunity for growth. Always embrace the chance to learn. By opening ourselves up to advice, ideas, or input from others, we allow ourselves to expand our knowledge, skills, and expertise. This is not to say that you need to agree or accept everything or anything at face value, but be open to it. Examine and explore everything with the realization that, regardless of how far you have come, there is still so much more to learn and experience. Emerson wrote, *"In every man there is something wherein I may learn, and in that I am his pupil."* This perceptive quote is a tribute to all people and events—that in each one, there is something to gain, discover or take away, sometimes as the pupil and others, as the teacher. This approach will help you experience life at its fullest, increase your options, and foster success.

Each day brings challenges to strengthen our resolve and opportunities to thrive, but we need to reach out for them. Never be discouraged or feel uncomfortable because you do not know something. Adopt that as opportunity to learn. Ask questions, be inquisitive, and always keep your mind open to new ideas or possibilities. Anything you encounter in your daily routine, whether meeting someone new, or collecting information, is a chance to grow and learn. Daniel Bell wrote, "*The most important attitude that can be formed is that of the desire to go on learning.*" The second we believe we are complete or have reached our potential, there is nowhere to go. The moment you think you know everything, understand you know relatively nothing—knowledge and information are infinite. If we consider ourselves green, we will grow; if we consider ourselves ripe, we will rot. Continually feed your mind with different ideas and insights.

> *You are your greatest investment. The more you store in that mind of yours, the more you enrich your experience, the more people you meet, the more books you read, the more places you visit, the greater is that investment in all that you are. Everything that you add to our peace of mind, and to your outlook upon life, is added capital that no one but yourself can dissipate.* – George Matthew Adams

Knowledge is omnipresent, all around us to gather and share. Lord Chesterfield wrote, "*There is hardly any place or any company where you may not gain knowledge.*" A great conversation is one that is equality balanced. Similar to a tennis match, it is a balanced exchange of ideas and information, sincere listening and giving—not a fencing match. Learn the power in being the pupil; one who seeks to learn and understand. When at school, spend some one-on-one time with the professors. Take advantage of their office hours to collect invaluable insight into a subject. Inquire about a topic and gain a more in-depth understanding. At work, find someone who specializes in a different field of interest. Initiate conversations. In essence, make an opportunity to learn something new every day. Family or friends hold an abundance of interesting facts, stories, and events that can enliven our minds and nourish our intellect. Imagine what could be accomplished with just an hour a day on a topic or subject.

Never develop a negative attitude or allow life to become redundant. Learn to challenge yourself daily and be open to new thoughts or discoveries. Find the power in even the smallest things. Life is extraordinary, if you work at it. Clutch onto the myriad of opportunities that are around us. Create a mindset to look for something interesting or informative daily. Learn a new subject, a language, or skill. Spend time reading about an issue or studying an interesting topic. Visit the library where you can get books, music, DVDs or books on tape to listen to in the car. With so much to achieve in the world, never allow yourself to become narrow minded or bogged down with excuses. Be receptive to others; for there is power in perception and amazing opportunity. Keep moving forward and take in everything you can. Momentum is vital in becoming stronger, smarter, and accomplishing your goals. Always learning and growing is an attitude—a forceful approach and mature outlook for conquering life, not being conquered by it.

I heard this story years ago at a lecture. It is about achieving great success even late in life; that age has no relevancy on fulfilling a dream—that it is never too late to start or learn something new. Regardless of time or circumstances, attitude and persistence can accomplish anything.

# Never Too Old to Learn

The famous entrepreneur Harland David Sanders, better known as Colonel Sanders, established his famous empire late in life. After years of different jobs and careers, he bought a service station when he was in his 40s and started serving chicken dishes and other meals for people who stopped by. As his popularity grew, Sanders opened up a restaurant and worked as a chef, spending years perfecting his chicken recipe. When the eventual construction of Interstate 75 diverted traffic from his restaurant, significantly cutting into his customer base, Sanders (at the time 65 years old) chose to move forward. When most people would be considering retirement, Sanders decided to grow his business. With little experience outside his own restaurant, he researched and studied the industry. He took $105.00 from his first Social Security check and tried to franchise his chicken to potential investors. He marched across the country looking for clients, but was continually rejected. Persistent, he continued to look for opportunities and learn from his experiences. After receiving over 1,000 rejections, he finally got a yes. From this, he continued his momentum and started building up his company. In 1964, Sanders sold his successful enterprise for over two million dollars. He continued on as its spokesperson for Kentucky Fried Chicken, collecting fees for his promotional visits and advertisements. He used some of his money to create the Colonel Harland Charitable Organization, which continues to aid charities and fund scholarships today. Sanders realized the importance of learning, and regardless of age, used his new found knowledge to build an empire.

# Always Learning and Growing

## Key Concepts and Focus

- Always embrace a chance to learn.

- In every moment or event, there is an opportunity to advance our knowledge.
- We need to be inquisitive and open ourselves up to advice and insights.
- Never be embarrassed to ask questions.
- If you always want to grow, be teachable and remain a pupil of life.

# 14

## *Flexibility and Adaptability*

*"The art of life is the constant readjustment to our surroundings."* – Kakuzo Okakaura

Although we may have a disciplined schedule and a solid plan for our life, we must remain flexible and adaptable to changes. By being too focused, we often miss the small opportunities that come along the way. We can also become frustrated if there are sudden setbacks or difficulties. We cannot know everything in life. Gears are always turning and circumstances are shifting, but we momentarily remain unaware of them until things suddenly appear or happen. Great opportunities can be easily missed if we are too rigid or inflexible. Louis Pasteur wrote, *"Chance favors the prepared mind."* Each day interesting developments emerge. Things not counted on or planned for can lead us further along our course and provide us with the direction needed. It could be an idea we were searching for, a person we wanted to meet, or the perfect prospect so badly needed. By keeping some sense of flexibility, we are predisposed to opportunity, moments of serendipity—a profound thought or a door suddenly opened that leads to further insight and progress.

Develop the ability and mindset to adapt to both internal and external changes. Remaining flexible can lead to more choices or a different approach to a problem. It can expedite an objective or offer profound insight. Niels Bohr wrote, "*Every great and deep difficulty bears in itself its own solution. It forces us to change our thinking in order to find it.*" Whether you are involved with a company, career, or family, things will happen and changes will occur. Be open to the circumstance, look for alternative solutions, and find the opportunity behind the problem. John Wooden wrote, "*An effective leader allows exceptions to the rule for exceptional results or when circumstance demands.*" Remain composed and be proactive. Keep alert and maintain some sense of flexibility in your daily life, for you never want to miss the solution to a problem or the road for which you have been searching.

Along with flexibility comes adaptability for changes in plans or events. Adaptability is a mental discipline that allows you to react quickly and productively when things happen. Doing what is necessary but never losing your focus or composure is a learned behavior. It helps to develop a propensity for acting with confidence and responsibility. In business and careers, those that can adapt to variations or new concepts succeed; those who remain committed to old systems fail. So many successful companies have imploded because they were not flexible to change and quick to adapt. Remaining static is an exercise in futility. Change is invaluable to keep in step with our rapidly advancing world, and we must be ready to adjust to the circumstances. Winston Churchill wrote, "*In life, it is often necessary when some cherished scheme has failed, to take up the best alternative.*" As new concepts or alternative solutions are presented, always be ready to readjust and modify your present method or technique. Perhaps you are moving to a new location, starting a different career, entering into a new relationship, or venturing somewhere you have never gone. Be flexible, and adapt to change. Those who succeed in life learn to adapt their talents and vision to changing circumstances. They are quick to learn new skills, look for alternative solutions, and find the best in any situation.

Richard Branson is a great example of someone who exemplifies flexibility and adaptability. He continues to adjust to changing times, makes the best out of difficult situations, takes risks for progress, and always creates different or new ways of doing things.

## *The Empire Builder*

Branson first started his company in 1970 (at age twenty) with a couple of friends and formed a small record mail-order business. The idea was to offer discounted prices and then send the record directly to the client. As things started to take off, the British postal service declared a strike throughout the country, jeopardizing his company. Branson remained flexible and adapted to the situation. He decided to open up a chain of record stores in 1972, Virgin Records. The shops offered a place where people could hang out, listen to music, and buy products. Then he decided to set up a recording studio where musicians could spend time working on their music. Although he lacked the resources, he purchased a country estate outside of London and soon started signing some bands under his own label (Virgin Records). Although many groups were unsuccessful, Virgin Records had a few hits, and profits started to come in. The company continued to grow and in 1992, he sold it for $1 billion dollars.

One of his next ventures was Virgin Airlines, founded in 1984. With only a few planes and cutthroat competition, he moved forward. Shortly after, a major fuel crisis threatened his new venture. Also, a competing airline attempted to purloin his customers to put him out of business. Branson remained flexible, adapted to each problem, took risks, and focused on the long term goals. He ended up leasing new planes, with the latest technology, and turned Virgin Airlines into a strong competitor. Through the entire process, there were many setbacks, cash flow problems, and economic changes; but Branson always looked for opportunities and adjusted to the situation. He founded over 360 businesses under the Virgin label. His estimated worth is approximately $4.4 billion dollars.

## *Flexibility and Adaptability*

### Key Concepts and Focus

- Always remain focused, but flexible—be open to new ideas and opportunities.
- Stay alert, and maintain some sense of flexibility in your daily life.
- When things change, be quick to adapt to new challenges or different environments.
- The more relaxed and flexible we remain, the more accessible our success.
- Those who succeed in life adapt their talents and vision to changing situations.

# 15

## *Expect Change*

*"When you are through changing, you are through."*
– Bruce Barton

As we go through life, change is inevitable. Therefore, we must be prepared at all times to adapt. Develop a sense of adventure so that when changes occur, you can meet them head on. Treat them as opportunities to grow and learn something new. You will start to experience life differently, expand your mind, and discover hidden talents as you encounter circumstances. Avoid forming an undermining belief that you have peaked or reached the end. Once we consider ourselves finished, we limit our possibilities or opportunities. There is no plateau or middle ground in life (although sometimes it may feel that way). If we do not go forward, we fall backwards. If we do not grow, we shrink. Goethe wrote, *"We must always change, renew, rejuvenate ourselves; otherwise we harden."* Regardless of age, we must continue to test ourselves and set higher expectations.

Always maintain a vision for the future and set your sights on following through. This provides a purpose for living and enables us to reach a greater potential. As you focus on your goals and move forward, expect change: new relationships formed, discouraging memories forgotten, knowledge expanded, difficult challenges accomplished, endurance strengthened, talents cultivated, your passion fostered; creativity enlightened; your character matured, and your mastery over the past. The cost of greatness is the ability to change, a very small price to pay for the benefits we receive.

Change is similar to athletics. If you start working out and get into a solid routine, you will notice physical and mental changes. You will lose weight, build stronger muscles, gain energy, and become more confident. If you work toward your objectives and remain focused on your goals, you will start to notice changes. You will find more purpose in life and passion for what you want, increased discipline, broadened expectations, heightened attitude, and the fostering of more ideas into action. Opportunities will begin to surface that lead you in the direction you desire.

> *We must drop the idea that change comes slowly. It does ordinarily—in part because we think it does. Today changes must come fast; and we must adjust our mental habits, so that we can accept comfortably the idea of stopping one thing and beginning another overnight. We must discard the idea that past routine, past ways of doing things are probably the best way. On the contrary, we must assume that there is probably a better way to do almost everything. We must stop assuming that a thing which has never been done before probably cannot be done at all.* – Donald M. Nelson

By staying focused and advancing forward, you are leaving the past. Even yesterday becomes a part of history. Seek what you desire with the confidence of receiving it and continue on until you have obtained it. Creating these expectations sets your mind in motion, fosters results, and brings change. Be prepared to see and experience everything differently as your world moves forward. With higher expectations, your standards increase. Improving daily brings continual experiences and wisdom, so anticipate new insights and events to transform. John F. Kennedy wrote, *"Change is the law of life and those who look only to the past or present are certain to miss the future."* Know that continued effort delivers progress, sometimes slight or not immediately noticeable; but if you look back after a week or month, you should observe genuine results. Similar to running a marathon, you start out with a mile and gradually increase. After a few weeks, you are up to three miles and maybe 10 after a month. Sometimes slowly, and sometime in great leaps, you are moving forward and improving, so be prepared for change. Have faith and feel the confidence and freedom this infuses— the excitement of becoming better and discovering new things. Personal development and growth are essential to experiencing a fulfilled and complete life. See what you want to become, and become it, but expect change.

## *Another Tack*

*When you suspect you're going wrong,*
*Or lack the strength to move along,*
*With placid poise among your peers,*
*Because of haunting doubts or fears:*
*It's time for you to shift your pack,*
*And steer upon another tack!*

*When wind and waves assail your ship,*
*And anchors from the bottom slip;*
*When clouds of mist obscure your sun,*
*And foaming waters madly run:*
*It's time for you to change your plan,*
*And make a port while yet you can!*

*When men laugh at your woeful plight,*
*And seek your old repute to blight;*
*When all the world bestows a frown,*

*While you are sliding swiftly down:*
*It's time for you to show your grit.*
*And let the scoffers know you are fit!*

*When Failure opens your luckless door,*
*And struts across the creaking floor;*
*When Fortune flees and leaves you bare,*
*And former friends but coldly stare:*
*It's time for you to take a tack,*
*And show the world you're coming back!*
- Lilburn Harwood Townsend

# Expect Change

## Key Concepts and Focus

- Change is a necessary characteristic of life.
- We are either moving forward or going backwards.
- Never allow life to become redundant or boring—challenge yourself daily.
- Anticipate new insights, developments, and events to transpire.
- See what you want to become, and become it, but expect change.

# 16

## *Be Prepared for Success*

*"Great minds have purpose; others have wishes."* – Washington Irving

Being ready for success stimulates the mental capacity to receive it. It prepares the mind, instills confidence through the process, and generates unexpected events and opportunities waiting to be seized. As you put together your strategy for the future and confidently move to accomplish it, be prepared for success physically, emotionally, and mentally. Connect with it, and believe it will happen. Visualize the entire outcome, what it will look like, and where you will go from there. So many determined people have failed because they were not prepared for success. Countless others reached their goals, but then found themselves lost without a further plan. We can never reach a goal until we first see it; so be specific and clear in what you want. Yogi Berra wrote, *"If you don't know where you're going, you'll end up somewhere else."* We must define our ambitions to achieve them and guide our mind in that direction.

Prepare for it every day. Do whatever is necessary to succeed. Make a list of the steps needed, people to talk to, and things that should be accomplished. Devote 10 or 20 minutes each morning to concentrate on your goals and connect with your desires.

John Henry Patterson wrote, "*You must make a habit of thinking in terms of a defined objective.*" The more time you spend on something, the more you will get out of it. If you want to run a marathon, you need to plan for the event: organize a diet, arrange a workout schedule, and start running every day. Train your mind for the event, and build on your confidence. Visualize yourself running through the course and finishing successfully. The same is true when preparing for your future. Run through events in your mind until they become second nature. Once you connect with them and envision what you want, work toward making them a reality. Charles Garfield wrote, "*I've discovered that numerous peak performers use the skill of mental rehearsal of visualization. They mentally run through important events before they happen.*" We must realize what we want to accomplish and focus on the end result.

Many things have been written about visualization; but whether you are familiar with it or not, it is one the most powerful and effective ways to transform the future and maximize results. Some of the most successful athletes, entrepreneurs, and leaders have used this method to enhance their abilities and reach their goals. The famous golfer Jack Nicklaus used visualization in preparing for competitive games. He would continually go over a shot in his mind before ever stepping onto the green. Nicklaus visualized the routine hundreds of times, seeing how he wanted to hit the ball, and where he wanted to put it. When he finally stepped up for the shot, he had already accomplished it. During the 1970s and 80s, the Russians perfected the use of visualization in sports; part of the reason they won so many gold medals and dominated the Olympics. They mentally saw themselves perfectly running through all the motions and succeeding in each event. When they actually approached the competition, they just followed through with what they already rehearsed. In one of the best known studies on visualization in sports, Russian scientists compared four groups of equally competitive Olympic athletes in terms of their training schedules:

- Group 1: 100% training
- Group 2: 75% training; 25% visualization
- Group 3: 50% training; 50% visualization
- Group 4: 25% training; 75% visualization

Group 4, with 75% of their time devoted to mental training, performed the best. The Soviets discovered that mental images can act as a prelude to muscular impulses. It is a process of preparing and programming the mind.

Whatever your ambitions, get your thoughts around them. Visualize the results you desire, and create an organized list of everything you need to accomplish it. Spending consistent time thinking about the future and working through it in your mind is essential. Create a detailed picture of your goals and the outcomes you want. Anything is possible, but you need to prepare for it. Research the subject as thoroughly as you can, get input from others, and do what is needed. Planning is the core; action is the key. Henry Hartman wrote, *"Success always comes when preparation meets opportunity."* If you want to change a job or career, start thinking about what you are good at. Catalog your talents and what others say you do well. Define your objective, and research the type of company you want to work for. Explore the subject, talk to people in the field, and take a class on the topic. Every day you move in that direction, you gain the knowledge and preparation you need. Whatever your objective, the more organized your thoughts and more thorough your plans, the clearer the results will become. See the end goal, and work backwards. The more time you spend, the greater the outcome.

> *Live your life each day as you would climb a mountain. An occasional glance toward the summit keeps the goal in mind, but many beautiful scenes are to be observed from each new vantage point. Climb slowly, steadily, enjoying each passing moment; and the view from the summit will serve as a fitting climax for the journey.* – Harold V. Melchert

When reflecting on your objectives, spend some of that time alone. In solitude, you can truly connect with your ideas and plans. Emerson wrote, "*Solitude is the safeguard against mediocrity.*" Wherever you may be, seclusion enables you to focus clearly on your ambitions without distractions. Create a time and place that offer you the environment needed. Learn to relax, and just concentrate on your goals. Sir Edward Gibbons wrote, "*Solitude is the school of genius.*" Having a clear mind will facilitate your thoughts and widen your vision. Your continual focus will create the direction desired and needed. The more specific you are, the better the outcome; the stronger your intentions, the faster the results. Simply work through your goals and objectives; move in that direction, and prepare yourself for success.

## *The Foundation of Success*

*The wisdom of preparation*
*The value of confidence*
*The worth of honesty*
*The privilege of working*

*The discipline of struggle*
*The magnetism of character*
*The radiance of health*
*The forcefulness of simplicity*
*The winsomeness of courtesy*
*The attractiveness of modesty*
*The satisfaction of serving*
*The power of suggestion*
*The buoyancy of enthusiasm*
*The advantage of initiative*
*The virtue of patience*
*The rewards of co-operation*
*The fruitfulness of perseverance*
*The sportsmanship of losing*
*The joy of winning*
- Rollo C. Hester

# *Prepare for Success*

## Key Concepts and Focus

- Readiness for success stimulates the mental capacity to receive it.
- Be prepared mentally, physically, and emotionally.
- Define your goals and visualize the outcome you desire.
- Whatever your objective, the more organized your thoughts, the more thorough your plans, the clearer the results will become.
- The stronger your intentions, the faster the results.

# Wisdom

17  *The Essence of Rest*

18  *Master Your Mornings*

19  *Learn to Relax*

20  *This Is the Best Time of Your Life*

21  *Giving and Receiving*

22  *Seizing Rare Moments*

23  *The Power of Simplicity*

# 17

# *The Essence of Rest*

*"Lose an hour in the morning, and you will be
all day hunting for it"* – Richard Whately

Mornings are the most important part of the day, for they set the tone and pace. Having a clear mind and a rested body is crucial for success. Being properly refreshed and alert before we start again is essential in maximizing our ability and performing at our best. Shakespeare described sleep as *"the chief nourisher in life's feast;" deep rest is necessary for keeping body, mind and spirit in good form."* Although some flourish at night, the morning is still a critical part of the day. It is when everyone starts and everything moves forward. Mornings give us another chance to start again, reconnect with our plans, and build on our momentum.

> Continued research shows that getting less than seven-to-eight hours of rest every night causes diminished cognitive performance and mental capacity. Sleep debt (deficient rest) causes mental, emotional, and physical fatigue. It affects the immune system, memory, and metabolism. Getting to sleep later or breaking your sleeping pattern

also has a profound effect on the quality of rest you receive. Even with the proper eight hours, going to sleep past 11 P.M. can often lower your performance the next day. Although alcohol may help in getting to sleep, too much will actually affect the quality of rest, regardless of eight or more hours. Research also shows that taking a nap or even laying down for 10-20 minutes with your eyes closed can help relax the body and rejuvenate the mind. Learn to listen to your body and give it the proper attention—it is often the best indicator of what you need.

Occasionally one can have a bad day, be exhausted, or lack clarity. Events go wrong, or things are out of our control. Often, when feeling like this, we make the mistake of trying to still move on; but feeling frustrated, we further add to the anxiety. We may end up making mistakes or bad decisions, doing something foolish, or just staying up too late; yet this can jeopardize tomorrow. No matter how hard we try, there will be times that just go nowhere. Although every day is important, sometimes just lie down, read, and go to sleep. Proper rest will help you relax and recharge for a better time tomorrow. Ernest Hemingway wrote, "*I still need more healthy rest in order to work at my best. My health is the main capital I have and I want to administer it intelligently.*" Understand the importance of rest and nourishing yourself with proper sleep. Your mind will be clearer and your body stronger. Harold J. Reilly wrote, "*Rest has cured more people than all the medicine in the world.*" It is always good to rally, do everything you can, and get the most out of each moment; but occasionally, just let it go and head to sleep. Tomorrow is another chance to excel.

# *Sleep*

*Sleep, a solace to all mortals*
*Sleep, to some so natural*
*Sleep, to many so elusive*
*Sleep, to some so simple*
*Sleep, to some a real struggle*
*Sleep, for some, bountiful to envy*
*Sleep, for some, commodity to buy*
*Sleep, in it some walk riskily*
*Sleep, in it some talk profusely*
*Sleep, a gift to all human beings*
*Sleep, a basic necessity of life*
*Sleep well, wake up refreshed,*
*Step on to face daily challenges*
- Rangarajan Kazhiyur Mannar

# *The Essence of Rest*

## Key Concepts and Focus

- Mornings give us another chance to start again, reconnect with our plans, and build on our momentum.
- Being properly rested and refreshed before we start again is essential in maximizing our ability.
- Never compromise the night at the sacrifice of tomorrow.
- With proper rest, our next day can be extraordinary.
- Learn to listen to your body and know when it is time to sleep.

# 18

## *Master Your Mornings*

*"Everything comes too late for those who
only wait." – Elbert Hubbard*

Mornings are vital in setting our daily plans and objectives.
They are essential to reconnecting with ourselves, because our
attitude will dictate the outcome of the day. An athlete never
runs without stretching or preparing. The same principle applies
to the mornings. We need to stretch our mind continually and
warm up. When lacking motivation, snap out of it and refocus.
Get excited about being up and moving forward, looking ahead to
what interesting things or events may happen. Marcus Aurelius
wrote, *"When you arise in the morning, think of what a precious
privilege it is to be alive."* Review your goals, read an inspiring
quote, take a quick walk, workout to stimulate your mind and
body, eat a proper meal, and most important, rehearse in your
mind what you want to accomplish. Specifically focus on your
objectives and the process of getting there: places you need to
go, who you need to contact, and any other obligations. These
10 to 20 minutes in the morning are absolutely crucial in setting
into motion what you want out of the day. Research on cognitive
performance shows that just spending one hour of visualization

can accomplish more than six-to-seven hours of work. This same principle applies to planning your day.

> By visualizing the specific goals you want to accomplish first thing in the morning, you connect these thoughts with your mind and set into motion your agenda for the day. The mind knows only what you tell it and what it receives. By programming it first thing in the morning, it will direct your thoughts to accomplishing what it has been told. It is similar to programming a navigational system. Regardless of the weather, the boat will keep its course. Another example is visiting a new city for the first time. If you study a map and plan everywhere you want to go, you will have the proper directions to get there with time to accomplish what you want. If you do not, you will get lost and waste time. What often happens as we rush into the day is that we become instantly saturated with other thoughts and distractions. It knocks us off course, and we end up in an entirely different place. Just one degree can set us off by miles.

By seeing what you want to do, you focus on what is important and help facilitate the process. Even taking 15 minutes to concentrate on your day can improve the entire outcome and increase results. William Blake wrote, *"Think in the morning, act in the noon, read in the evening, and sleep at night."* This is a very simply process. Just spend a moment writing a list, and rehearse it a few times so you are clear about what you want to achieve. Then run through the events in the order you see them. Walk through each action in your mind. Visualize yourself conquering a difficult task or giving a presentation to clients or colleagues.

Many successful people realize there is a small window of time they can control: a moment to plan the day, read up on material, return e-mails, and set everything into motion. First thing in the morning, our mind is fresh and more receptive— with few distractions or interruptions. As things progress, we get sidetracked by other commitments and obligations. Squandering time and cluttering our thoughts leads only to frustration and wasted energy. Goethe wrote, *"Beware of dissipating your powers; strive constantly to concentrate them."* Concentrating on our goals makes a larger impact on our thoughts than the events that unfold throughout the day. Do whatever is necessary to create some extra time. If you need to get up earlier, do it. Setting a positive pattern every morning will discipline your mind to accomplish more.

If we know where we are going, we never waste any time getting there. Even when unexpected events occur, our earlier planning guides us through the day. As we move with momentum throughout the week, we still need the routine of going over our goals first thing. Set a schedule for yourself—a moment of focus and motivation. Create a list of all the activities, calls, and events you seek to accomplish. Make it ambitious, for you will accomplish more than conceived. Even as the day comes to an end, things still fit into place. If you are running late, take a breath, relax, and concentrate on your daily objectives. Next time, however, give yourself more time to allow for the unexpected. Always be attuned to your surroundings, looking for advantages and opportunity. Your day will be far more successful when you are ready and prepared.

# *A Creed*

*To be so strong that nothing can disturb your peace of mind; to talk health, happiness and prosperity; to make your friends feel that there is something in them; to look on the sunny side of everything; to think only of the best; to be just as enthusiastic about the success of others as you are about your own; to forget the mistakes of the past and profit by them; to wear a cheerful countenance and give a smile to everyone you meet; to be too large for worry, too noble for anger, too strong for fear, and too happy to permit the presence of trouble.*

- Christina D. Larson

# *Master Your Mornings*

## Key Concepts and Focus

- Mornings set the momentum for the entire day.
- If we know where we are going, we never waste any time getting there.
- Get into a routine of spending 15 to 20 minutes every morning planning the day.
- Review your goals and objectives and visualize what needs to be done.
- Start or continue some form of physical exercise, for this awakens the body, gets the blood flowing, and sets the pace for the day.
- Your day will be far more successful when you are ready and prepared.

# 19

## *Learn to Relax*

*"Tension is who you think you should be. Relaxation
is who you are."* – Chinese proverb

We choose our attitude and how to react during the day.
Whether we remain calm or lose our composure is up to us.
Getting anxious, frustrated, or angry is common practice, but
can be controlled. Choose to be uncommon, but extraordinary.
Frantically running around, getting upset, and yelling at others
has become acceptable behavior. This approach, however,
accomplishes nothing and is disrespectful to those around us.
It drives people away and embarrasses those who do it. Albert
Einstein wrote, *"Weakness of attitude becomes weakness of
character."* Becoming upset never helps us overcome a problem
or move forward productively. It wastes our energy and often
undermines an entire day or week. Regardless of the tension or
stress caused by a situation, remain calm and learn to relax.

In reflecting back, many things that brought us distress had
little value or importance, yet they robbed us of that moment.
Elwood Hendricks wrote, *"The price of anger is failure."* Never
waste time on frustration. Catch yourself when you feel
overwhelmed or distressed, and take a minute to recoup. Walk
away for a moment and collect your thoughts. By gathering

your composure, you will accomplish your tasks more efficiently. Those who keep calm, regardless of the circumstances, earn respect and can lead others through difficulties. Whether at home or in the office, remember to take a breath, refocus, and calmly move forward. Every time tension strikes, strike back. Practice the three Cs: *calm, cool and collected.* With these, you can successfully conquer anything. Save your day by refocusing for a minute or coming back to a problem later. Nothing is worth the price of anger.

Establishing a balanced life is essential. What we do to relax helps bring stability to our mind and body. Working too much or continually becoming overwhelmed by events simply adds tension and stress. Create time for yourself to enjoy the week: take a walk, play a sport, or do something you really like. Find something new or interesting. Even in the simplest things one can find enjoyment and contentment. Think about what you love doing. Whether tennis, golf, running, watching a movie, going out with friends, listening to music, taking a drive, or visiting somewhere new, just do it. These interludes are just as important as work or other responsibilities. Getting out and having fun can clear the mind and improve our outlook and performance. It rejuvenates our spirit and provides stability. Relaxation calms our stress and puts everything in perspective. Learn to balance obligations with fun and enjoyment—moments where you can reconnect with your thoughts, open up your mind to ideas or allow opportunity to approach. You will accomplish more in a day by remaining calm and composed, so learn to relax and spend some time doing the things you love.

*To laugh often and much;*
*To win the respect of intelligent people*
*and the affection of children;*
*To earn appreciation of honest critics*
*and endure the betrayal of false friend;*
*To appreciate beauty,*
*to find the best in others;*

*To leave the world a bit better,*
*whether by a healthy child,*
*a garden patch,*
*or a redeemed social condition;*
*To know even one life has breathed easier because you have lived.*
*This is to have succeeded!*
- Ralph Waldo Emerson

# *Learn to Relax*

## Key Concepts and Focus

- Whether we remain calm or lose our composer is up to us.
- We chose our attitude and how to react during the day.
- By remaining calm and relaxed, we accomplish more in everything we do.
- Establishing a balanced life is essential for fulfillment and success.
- Create time for yourself to enjoy the week.  Take a walk, play a sport, or do something you really like.
- Find what brings you pleasure and pursue it.

# 20

## *This Is the Best Time of Your Life*

*"What is there to do with life but to live
it to the full."* – Arnold Glasow

Although an entire lifetime is ahead of you, filled with hopes and ambitions, remember to make the most out of today. Too often we focus on the future or what we want to become and forget about living in the moment. While it is imperative to have goals and objectives, never forget about having fun and enjoyment today. Seize the hour, the morning, the night and get everything you can out of it. Og Mandino wrote, *"Live this day as if it will be your last. Remember that you will only find "tomorrow" on the calendars of fools. Forget yesterday's defeats and ignore the problems of tomorrow ... Make it the best day of your year."*

Excitement and inspiration can often appear where least expected. What may seem as another common day can be filled with spectacular moments or opportunity: a conversation that stimulates the mind; an encouraging word; a peaceful walk that inspires the soul; meeting a friend; setting a goal; breaking a past record; a brilliant sunset; an exhilarating workout; a new relationship; a bold resolution; a decision that changes your life; an ambitious move; a glorious attempt, or seeing something differently. These simple opportunities surround us daily, but are often missed because we become consumed with concerns or commitments. Regardless of the past or future, today is what counts.

This focus is not to be misunderstood regarding, perhaps, a very difficult time in your life, whether you are going through a severe hardship or the loss of someone close. However, it is a general rule of thought about living for today and making it count. Even in the worst of times, there can be amazing moments of peace or excitement: an inspiring word of support, clear insight into the future, a revelation. Take the initiative and always make the most of each day. Never think what the moment is not, but what it offers right now. So many people prepare themselves for life, but never really live. Do not allow time to escape you or waste the day squandering valuable hours. One of the greatest regrets people have is that they never risked enough or took a chance, or waited too long. Yesterday is the past, and what is tomorrow may never come. When was the last time you took a day off, reconnected with an old relationship, forged a new friendship, or did something daring? Have confidence in yourself and be bold. Stay focused on your goals, but enjoy the ride along the way. Be daring and take some risks.

> *Do more than exist, live.*
> *Do more than touch, feel.*
> *Do more than look, observe.*
> *Do more than read, absorb.*
> *Do more than hear, listen.*
> *Do more than listen, understand.*
> *Do more than think, ponder.*
> *Do more than talk, say something.*
> - John H. Rhoades

In thinking this is the best time of your life, you change your perspective, stimulate your mind, and open yourself to opportunity. You are not settling for less or compromising your ambitions, but it allows you to form the necessary attitude to enjoy your time no matter what happens. Never let circumstances rob this from you. The power in appreciation dissipates sorrow, instills confidences, and produces success. Maria Robinson wrote, "*Nobody can go back and start a new beginning, but anyone can start today and make a new ending.*" Living today never takes away from moving toward your dreams. It just makes the journey more extraordinary. Most of life truly is the journey—what we do and whom we meet along the way. The power of choice, understanding that today is ours, brings another chance to excel. Confront life and get everything you can out of it; experience each moment to its fullest. Focus on where you are right now, and make the day incredible. Do something different, challenging, and special. This is the gift you have, so never let anything take that away. The opportunity is always there if you seize it.

## *The Person You Are*

*It isn't the one that you might have been*
*Had the chance been yours again,*
*Nor the prize you wanted but didn't win*
*That weights in the measure of men.*
*No futile "if" or cowardly "because"*
*Can rowel your stock to par*
*The world cares naught for what never was—*
*It judges by what you are.*

*It isn't the person that you hope to be,*
*If fortune and fate are kind,*
*That the chill, keen eyes of the world will see,*
*In weighing your will and mind.*
*The years ahead are a chartless sea,*
*And tomorrow's a world away;*
*It isn't the person that you'd like to be,*

*But the one that you are today.*

*There's little worth in the phantom praise*
*Of a time that may never dawn,*
*And less in a vain regret for days*
*And deeds long buried and gone.*
*There's little time on this busy earth*
*To argue the why and how.*
*The game is yours if you prove your worth,*
*And prove it here and now!*
- Ted Olsen

# *This Is the Best Time of Your Life*

## Key Concepts and Focus

- Make each day count and live in the moment.
- Seize the hour, the morning, the night and get everything you can out of it.
- Challenge yourself daily to see something new, learn something different, or do something unique or daring.
- Always embrace those whom you care about and let them know each day.
- Living today never takes away from moving toward your dreams.  It just makes the journey more extraordinary, and most of life truly is the journey.

# 21

## *Giving and Receiving*

*"Behave towards everyone as if receiving a great guest."*
– Confucius

Giving to others is a simple yet powerful principle of life; a law of nature that cannot be ignored and should always be embraced. No one ever gets to the top or succeeds alone. If anyone did, they would want to leave once they got there. We all owe parts of our life to others and what they gave: their generosity, influence, opportunity, wisdom, direction, insight, support, kindness, and love. Lord Byron wrote, *"All who would win joy, must share it."* Everyone has experienced people who have helped and influenced them. Think of a friend whose devotion guided you through a troubled time and pushed you forward: a professor or teacher who had a profound effect on your learning; someone at work whose guidance helped your career. Whether stranger or friend, many people, seen and unseen, help and impact our daily lives. Extraordinary miracles that go on behind the scenes unnoticed, such as acts of kindness or compassion, those working on our behalf and providing something of themselves— this is the thread woven through society that keeps everything together and gives life purpose.

Life is about people and giving what we can. True power comes from treating others with respect and thoughtfulness. If you ever want to improve your current situation or future prospects, start giving a part of yourself to others. Get involved in a group, charity, or someone else's life. Whether it is support, advice, money, or just compassion, a little of our time can make an enormous impact. Winston Churchill wrote, "*We make a living by what we get, we make a life by what we give.*" Oh, the power and force that kindness creates! Boredom is alleviated, complacency lifted, sorrow lightened, purpose fostered, confidence gained, enthusiasm restored, efforts rewarded, opportunity found, guidance given, and prosperity increased.

> *A happy life is made up of little things in which smiles and small favors are given habitually. A gift sent, a letter written, a call made, a recommendation given, transportation provided, a book lent, a check sent— things that are done without hesitation. Kindness isn't sacrifice so much as it is being considerate for the feelings of others, sharing happiness, the unselfish thought, the spontaneous and friendly act, forgetfulness of our own present interests.* – Carl Holmes

Giving comes in many forms and is the essential balance to life. Nothing is ever gained by acting with regret or selfishness. Feeling bitterness or discontent only compromises our present and future. We all have the capacity to make decisions; and if some of these were wrong, if we were misguided or taken advantage of, learn to forgive yourself and others. To blame people for mistakes or hold them responsible for failure is our own failure. Let go of these debilitating feelings, and replace them with compassion and understanding. Those who are ruthless in business or in life are common enough. Any success they have achieved was built on sand and will eventually wash away. Yet people will be people, and everyone makes mistakes.

It is within our power to choose how we act and move forward. Feel the strength that comes from giving forgiveness. Although it may not be easy, often taking the hard road is the right road. Anything that comes too easily, is valued too lightly.

Open your life to the excitement and opportunity that comes from being kind and giving. Develop the attitude and fortitude of encouraging people instead of putting them down; to see where one might need help and provide it; to be the friend you would like to have. William Boetcker wrote, "*Your greatness is measured by your kindness.*" Often a kind smile, a thoughtful hello, or a nice gesture can make an enormous impact on someone. Opportunities abound in a single day, and we should take advantage of as many as we can. What we desire, we attract; what we sow, we reap; whatever we put in, we get back. By acting with compassion and love, we receive all in return. Unselfish actions produce incredible results. One complement to someone can last their entire life. If each of us were to go out and touch one individual's life, getting involved in one productive way every week, it would transform their world as well as ours. It starts with one person at a time and becomes a ripple effect. You never know what one act can do. You can often change a person's life with just one encouraging word or act of compassion.

I first heard this true story about 15 years ago. It left a lasting impression on how someone's life can be so influenced and changed by giving a little help and guidance when needed, how such a small incident could have such a large impact. It also speaks volumes on how impressionable children are and how a little kindness can make an enormous difference. It is simple in context, but powerful in principle.

# *One Person Can Make a Difference*

She was a fifth-grade school teacher by the name of Miss Thompson, and every year when she met with her new students, she would say to them, *"Boys and girls, I love you all the same and I have no favorites."* Of course she wasn't being completely truthful. Teachers do have favorites, and what's worse, most teachers have students that they just don't like. Well, Teddy Staller was a boy that Miss Thompson just didn't like, and for good reason; he didn't seem at all interested in school. He had a deadpan blank expression on his face; and glassy, unfocused eyes. His clothes were musky, and his hair unkempt. He wasn't an attractive boy, and he certainly wasn't likeable. When Miss Thompson marked Teddy's papers, she got kind of a perverse pleasure out of putting Xs next to the wrong answers. When she put Fs at the top of his paper, she did it with a flare. She should have known better. She had Teddy's records, so she knew more about him then she wanted to admit. His records read like this:

> **First grade:** Teddy shows promise with his work and attitude, but he has a poor home situation. **Second grade:** Teddy could do better. His mother is seriously ill and he receives little help at home. **Third grade:** Teddy is a good boy, but too serious. He is a slow learner; his mother died this year. **Fourth grade:** Teddy is very slow but well behaved; his father shows no interest.

Well, when Christmas came, the boys and girls brought Miss Thompson Christmas gifts. They piled the presents on her desk and crowded around to watch her open them. Among the gifts was one from Teddy Staller. She was surprised that he had brought her a present. Teddy's gift was wrapped in brown paper and held together with scotch tape. Written on the front were the simple words: *For Miss Thompson, From Teddy.* When she unwrapped the present, out fell an ugly looking rhinestone bracelet, with half the stones missing, and a bottle of cheap perfume. The other boys and girls began to giggle and smirk over Teddy's gift. But at least Miss Thompson had enough sense to silence them by immediately attaching the bracelet to her wrist and putting on some perfume. As she held out her arm for all the others to see, she said, *"Doesn't the perfume smell lovely?"* Taking her cue, the children began to say, *"Oh yeah, it really does smell good."*

At the end of the day when school was over and all the other students went home, Teddy lingered behind. He slowly walked over to her desk and softly said, *"Miss Thompson, Miss Thompson. You smell just like my mother does and her bracelet really looks pretty on you. I'm so glad you like my presents."* When Teddy left, Miss Thompson was deeply convicted. She got down on her knees and asked God to forgive her. The next day she started on a mission that she never before had in her life. She was now committed to teaching those children, especially Teddy Staller. She worked with him after school and gave him all the extra help he needed. She taught him to such an extent that he not only caught up with most of the students, but passed others. After he left her class, she did not hear from him for a while until one day she received a letter in the mail which read:

> *"Dear Miss Thompson: I will be graduating second in my class and I wanted you to be the first to know. Love, Teddy Staller."*

> Four years later another letter came, which read: *"Dear Miss Thompson: I will be graduating first in my class. The university was hard, but I liked it. Love, Teddy Staller."*

> Four years later she received yet another letter, which read: *"Dear Miss Thompson: as of today, I am Theodor Staller, M.D., how about that. I'm getting married next month, the tenth to be exact, and I want you to come to the wedding. Father died last month and you're all the family I got left."*

Miss Thompson went to that wedding and sat where Teddy's mother would have sat; she deserved to. She did something for him that he would never forget.

# *Giving and Receiving*

## Key Concepts and Focus

- Giving to others is a simple yet powerful principle of life—a law of nature that cannot be ignored and should always be embraced.
- Treat others as you would like to be treated.
- Be aware of people in your life and always act with respect and kindness.
- Know that just one kind or encouraging word can change a person's life.
- Try to give something of yourself every day to at least one other person.

# 22

## *Seizing Rare Moments*

*"Ability has nothing to do with opportunity."* – Napoleon Bonaparte

Too often we get so wrapped up in our daily lives that we miss incredible opportunities and wonderful experiences that are in front of us. By remaining too focused or consumed with problems, we overlook the very essence of what we are living for. Every day offers profound and extraordinary moments if we are consciously prepared to receive them. Within the framework of rigorous schedules and disciplined momentum are amazing events occurring around us. Abraham Lincoln wrote, *"In the end, it's not the years in your life that count. It's the life in your years."* Whether it is a challenging career or demanding home life, we become overwhelmed and forget to pause to take in the rare moments of simplicity, laughter, happiness, and gratitude. We need to realize when an opportunity exists and embrace it. They are constant, yet too often missed.

Life is not always measured by success or wealth, but by what we did to get there, those moments of excitement and inspiration along the way—small victories won or a goal accomplished. We spend so much time climbing to the top of the mountain; we never pause to look at the view. We tend to miss so much: the scenery around us, the friends we could have met, the things we could have learned, and quality time with a loved one. Years later we look back and realize how many of those wonderful experiences slipped by us without even noticing. Create time for yourself to pursue the things you enjoy, and spend time with those you love. Relax and enjoy your life along the journey. Practice stillness and open up your mind to the moment. If we want to move forward, we must appreciate where we are now.

> *A Creed:*
> *I would be true,*
> *For there are those who trust me;*
> *I would be pure,*
> *For there are those who care;*
> *I would be strong,*
> *For there is much to suffer;*
> *I would be brave,*
> *For there is much to dare;*
> *I would be a friend to all—*
> *The foe—the friendless;*
> *I would be giving,*
> *And forget the gift;*
> *I would be humble,*
> *For I know my weakness;*
> *I would look up—*
> *And laugh—and love—and lift.*
> - Howard A. Wheeler

Never become overwhelmed by circumstances or situations that may never happen. Often, what may appear to be an extraordinary problem is, in fact, a wonderful opportunity. Sometimes even the most difficult situations are miraculous occasions for change. Charles Swindoll wrote, "*We are all faced with a series of great opportunities brilliantly disguised as impossible situations.*" Discover the art of taking a subject or problem off the shelf, doing everything you can, then putting it in a place where it does not continually return to influence you. Never allow distractions to interfere with those perfect and peaceful moments waiting to be seized. Put things into their proper prospective. Learn to compose your thoughts, set concerns aside, and enjoy the hour or day. Make time to reflect, have fun, and enjoy your family. Spend time with your children, inspire a friend, or do something exciting after work. Create a proper balance in your life. Be in the moment and experience life to its fullest. Appreciate where you are right now, and be open to what each day offers.

Although Albert Einstein is known for his amazing discoveries and contributions to science, he was someone who appreciated the simplest things in life. Einstein found contentment in walking and examining nature. He continually asked questions and looked at things from a different view point.

# *A Powerful Mind*

After graduating from the Swiss Federal Institute of Technology in Zurich, with a degree in physics, Einstein struggled to find a teaching position or fulltime job. In the meantime he tutored students in math and science. After two years, he finally landed a position as a patent clerk in Bern, Switzerland. The position had little to do with physics or teaching, but Einstein seized the opportunity. After finishing his daily requirements, he spent the rest of the time experimenting with his concepts and writing down ideas. He would conduct thought experiments and work through his theories. Einstein soon formed a fellowship with two other scholars and created his own club: *The Olympia Academy*. The men would consume the night reading philosophy books, discussing topics, and developing concepts. Many of Einstein's greatest thoughts came out of these simple experiences. He made the best of his situation and seized these rare moments.

In 1905, he had four papers published. One was his landmark theory of relativity. Although some leading academics saw his paper as a major achievement, job offers still eluded him; and Einstein remained a clerk for years. Not until 1911 did Einstein receive an associate professorship at the University of Zurich, a less than adequate position for such a prominent intellectual. Finally in 1922, Einstein was awarded the Nobel Prize in Physics and became an international phenomenon. He traveled the world, gave lectures, and continued his studies. Although he is considered one of the most influential people in human history, he still loved to relax and enjoy the simplicity of life. In the smallest moments, he would find the greatest pleasures and made some of the most astounding discoveries.

## *Seizing rare Moments*

### Key Concepts and Focus

- By remaining too consumed with problems, we overlook the very essence of what we are living for.
- Every day offers extraordinary moments if we are prepared to seize them.
- Always be aware of your surroundings and look for opportunities.
- Even in the simplest things there can be extraordinary experiences.
- Find something new and interesting each day.

# 23

# *The Power of Simplicity*

*"Only those who have the patience to do simple
things perfectly will acquire the skill to do
difficult things easily." –* Johann Schiller

Realize the power in simple actions; that a thought, phone call,
or conversation could change your life. What is often deemed
as insignificant or irrelevant can be the very foundation of an
empire. M. Russell Ballard wrote, *"Small events and choices
determine the direction of our lives."* In everything we do, it is
about quality not quantity. In the smallest actions, extraordinary
things can come. Similar to planting a few seeds, one never
knows which ones will grow, but just one seed can produce
incredible results. Remain open and flexible; be receptive
to ideas or concepts. One thought or moment can turn into a
profound experience: the beginning of something amazing, the
final piece of a puzzle, a conversation that offers the guidance
needed, an idea that leads to a breakthrough, a small project
that provides a larger opportunity, the right timing that begins a
career, a simple event that brings prosperity, or the beginning of
a relationship that flourishes into something special.

Many successful people began their careers or companies
with one idea or event. It started with a simple concept that

became an action: a thought that became a book, an article that became a magazine, a story that became a movie, a melody that became a symphony, a canvas that became a painting, a small shop or business that became an empire, a creative product that became a global phenomena, a conversation that developed into a new theory, a different approach that revolutionized technology, a dream that became a reality. Everyone started somewhere, and most of the time it was with just a simple attempt or idea. Victor Hugo wrote, *"There is one thing stronger than all the armies in the world, and that is an idea whose time has come."* We must remain perceptive and alert in everything we do. Never compromise a day or a moment, for anything can come from it. Often in the smallest details are brilliant opportunities waiting to be seized—the beginning of something new and amazing.

While small details are important, so are large responsibilities. Sometimes we feel overwhelmed with daunting events or projects, but in these circumstances we can grow the strongest. Our abilities are stretched to the next level, and we start to realize what we are capable of. Never fall back when you have an opportunity to seize something challenging. David O. McKay wrote, *"Find a purpose in life so big it will challenge every capacity to be at your best."* It is far better to take on an opportunity bigger than yourself than to remain timid and lose out on the chance to grow. If you have the occasion to tackle something substantial, seize it and trust in yourself. You will be surprised how your mind and body rise to occasion—what is inside you waiting to flourish. Remain confident while you tackle the objective. Break it up into sections if necessary, and then put the whole thing together. Once you begin, you will be amazed how far you can and will progress. William DeMille wrote, *"I have always admired the ability to bite off more than one can chew and then chew it."* During these great moments, all of your faculties and abilities are utilized; your character nurtured and talent maximized. Soon you will discover the things that were a struggle for you actually become easier. What once seemed impossible, is now achievable. Know that you can accomplish anything you put your mind to.

## *From One Small Event*

An incredible event and a memorable journey began in a small town on the outskirts of Chicago. In one of the snow covered houses sat Tom watching television. He was up later than usual, but tonight there was something on the news that captivated him. The announcer was standing in the middle of the city reporting about the trouble with the homeless. In the background was a man freezing on a bench. Tom felt so moved by what he saw; he knew something must be done without delay. He ran to his room, and put a pillow under one arm and a blanket under the other. He got a ride downtown, peering out the window until he spotted the location he had seen. As Tom got out, he saw a man shivering on a wooden bench and approached him. Tom handed the man the blanket and said *"Here sir, this is for you."* The man smiled, then Tom handed him the pillow. With that, the man's eyes lit up and he replied, *"Thank you."*

Tom was so moved by the experience that he was determined to do more. The next day he made up flyers asking for help and distributed them all around his town. The neighbors thought it a bit strange at first, but Tom's continued enthusiasm inspired them to get involved. They organized groups of people to gather supplies and filled Tom's garage with blankets, pillows, and food. A neighbor down the street donated a van so everything could be carried into the city. Then a group of women started cooking meals to be taken along. Within a few weeks, the entire town was participating in a variety of capacities. Eventually shelters started popping up everywhere, bringing hope and a future to the homeless. This entire event began with just a simple gesture; a small occurrence that grew into an extraordinary event. What is most incredible about this true story of what one person started is that Tom was only eleven years old.

# *The Power of Simplicity*

## Key Concepts and Focus

- What is often deemed as insignificant or irrelevant can be the very foundation of something great.
- Many successes in life began with one idea or event. It started with a simple concept that became a powerful action.
- Large opportunities are fostered through small events.
- Tackle something difficult in your life, and use all of your capacity and skills to accomplish it.
- Often one small seed can lead to a great accomplishment.

# Responsibility

24  *Leading Others*

25  *Facing the Truth*

26  *You Are What You Eat*

27  *The Necessity of Physical Activity*

# 24

## *Leading Others*

*"Leadership is practiced not so much in words as in attitude and in action."* – Harold S. Geneen

Leadership is the most needed quality of the new millennium: character driven people who take control of situations and manage events for the improvement and benefit of others. Although the concept of leadership often denotes someone in the position of great power or authority, we all have the capacity to lead. Whether it is a company, position, or family, the quality and ability of leadership is essential. Donald H. McGannon wrote, *"Leadership is action, not position."* Unfortunately, too many do not grasp the fine distinction of leadership and end up compromising their standards and beliefs. In many situations, it is a grey area where the difference between right and wrong has been manipulated. Too many compromises are made in the attempt to please everyone. They fail to take a stand for what they firmly believe in and allow others to influence their decisions. This can happen at a corporation, in a business situation, at work, with friends, or in a relationship. In trying to succeed or produce results, we often move away from what we really believe in. We lower our standard instead of doing what we know is right. Yet true leadership is about being honest with ourselves and others and never compromising our ethics or values.

True leaders understand the importance of their position and never take advantage of it. They lead by example and conviction without hypocrisy; remain calm and composed in the heat of the moment; stay focused when others panic; take the blame when others cower; have the courage to make difficult decisions and stand behind them; are willing to make mistakes and move forward; bring out the best in others; stay optimistic, while solving problems; resolve complex issues, yet remain humble; communicate clearly and listen to others; do not seek self glory to cultivate their own selfish ambitions, but put others before themselves. We must stand firm for what we believe in and not allow ourselves to waiver like gusts of wind tossing us from one side to the other in an instant. Always remain strong and have confidence in yourself; trust your instincts and act with compassion, yet resolve.

> *Trained and inspired leadership is needed in the troubled world of today. We live in uncertainty and fear. The times call for thinking and straight thinking—one of the goals of true education. Unfortunately, the world so clamors for action that men and women devote little time to thinking. Many believe in second-hand thinking. They find it easier to ascertain and adopt the thoughts of others than to think for themselves.* – James F. Byrnes

The dictionary describes leadership as the *act to guide and direct people; to take control and lead others.* Three of the most important and fundamental characteristics of leadership are 1) integrity, 2) respect and 3) communication.

1. *Integrity* means veracity and reliability—no hypocrisy. It is a consistency of actions, values, methods, and

principles; a value system that one acts on and is always consistent with those actions. People with integrity are honest and trustworthy. They have a strong sense of ethics and always do what is right regardless of the circumstances. They respect others and treat people with consideration. They never contradict themselves and can be depended upon to do what they say. Honesty is the foundation, and their word is their bond.

2. *Respect.* Leaders understand the value of people and communicate this to them. They place an importance on those around them and the people they work with. They are sincere and treat others with dignity. They convey understanding and know the significance of building strong relationships. One can have all the information in the world or the greatest skills, but if they lack respect for others, the information and ability become useless.

3. *Communication.* Clear and consistent communication is central to leadership. Leaders are strong communicators and never assume others know what they are thinking. They let people know their intentions and continually inform others. They are good listeners and get feedback. For them, everyone's view point or opinion matters.

Leaders appreciate the privilege of position and never take advantage of it; never take others for granted or use people for their own gain. They know the importance of treating others with respect and bringing out the best in those around them— inspiring people and guiding them to success. Robert Half wrote, *"People who look down upon other people don't end up being looked up to."* They are steadfast and earn respect through acts of kindness and compassion; seize difficult moments and immediately attack problems; take control of circumstances and offer solutions, not excuses. William Boetcker wrote, a leader *"will never complain about the stupidity of his helpers, the ingratitude of mankind, nor the in-appreciation of the public.*

*These are all a part of the great game of life. To meet them and overcome them and not to go down before them in disgust, discouragement, or defeat—that is the final proof of power."* Whether playing a sport, working with a group of people, or being responsible for a family, have the confidence to take charge and lead; stay true to your beliefs, and never lower your standards. Always remain flexible and understand everyone's opinion or position. Have the character and fortitude never to waiver from your values and stay true to yourself.

One of the greatest stories I had ever read was about Ernest Shackleton. Even to this day, his incredible courage and character during the worst of circumstances is hard to fathom. He embodies the true idea of leadership, taking responsibility and doing whatever is necessary for the safety and preservation of others. His real story comes alive with the drastic failure of his 1914 expedition.

## *A Triumphant Failure*

Ernest Shackleton was born in Ireland in 1875. Bored with school, Shackleton left at 16 to join the Merchant Marines and by age 23 was certified as a Master Mariner, qualifying him to command a British ship anywhere in the world. He set out on a few arctic voyages and soon earned the respect and popularity of other sailors as a confident and strong leader. Shackleton achieved early success in 1907 for marching the farthest South latitude from the South Pole and was knighted by Edward VII. Yet Shackleton had loftier ambitious. Determined to make his mark in history, he soon turned his attention to the one remaining conquest—crossing the southern arctic continent from sea to sea. After carefully planning the 1,800-mile trip and recruiting the best men, he set out for victory in 1914. On December 5, he sailed his ship, the Endurance, from South Georgia Island toward Vahsel

Bay, Antarctic, but soon encountered sea ice. By January 19, 1915, the ship became frozen in the ocean. After months of waiting it out, the Endurance was crushed by the ice and the ship finally sank on November 21, 1915.

Faced with the reality that his conquest was over, he immediately changed his plans. Shackleton was no longer focused on the fame of exploration, but was instead determined to get every man home alive. He rallied their spirits and kept them busy with productive activities. The group then spent two months marching toward Paulet Island, but failed to reach it. The ice began to break up, and Shackleton's crew was forced into their three small life boats. Exhausted and tired, they sailed for five days and finally landed on Elephant Island, an inhospitable and desolate place. The island was far from any shipping routes or help, and Shackleton knew that time was against them. While he planned his next move, he organized the men and kept them busy. Shackleton knew their only hope was for a few men to somehow reach South Georgia Island over 800 miles away and get help.

Using the largest lifeboat and adding a few improvements, Shackleton carefully planned his strategy. He stored three weeks of supplies and picked his five best men for the impossible journey. They launched on April 24 and for fifteen horrific days, battled the most dangerous ocean known to sailors. After a terrible storm, they remarkably landed on South Georgia Island, but on the wrong side. Their only hope was to attempt a land crossing and reach the sailing port on the other side—something no one had ever done before. Shackleton traveled with two other companions through the freezing snow and up mountainous cliffs. After 36 straight hours, the men remarkably reached the whaling station at Stromness, north side. Desperate to save the rest of his men, he sailed out of the port; but his first three attempts were foiled by sea ice, blocking the approaches to the Elephant Island. Finally on August 30, 1917, Shackleton reached the island and quickly evacuated all 22 men. He kept his word. He saved every man and got them home safely. Although it was not the victory he was looking for, his name is etched in history for his overwhelming determination and successful leadership.

# *Leading Others*

## Key Concepts and Focus

- Everyone possesses the quality and capacity for leadership.
- Regardless of position, there are always opportunities to be a strong leader.
- The most effective leaders are those who:
  d. *Act with integrity and honor*
  e. *Treat others with respect and bring out their best qualities*
  f. *Stay focused and calm even in a crisis*
  g. *Never blame people for their mistakes*
  h. *Know what needs to be done and do it*

# 25

## *Facing the Truth*

*"Honesty is the first chapter in the book
of wisdom." –* Thomas Jefferson

Honor and truth are the foundations of character. An honest person can accomplish anything, for there are no boundaries or limits. Yet ignoring or dismissing the truth is easily done in forms of embellishing facts, manipulating information, or hiding unpleasant details. In moving forward and setting goals for your life, make sure to be honest with yourself and others. Everyone has endured uncomfortable moments or unfortunate circumstances, yet there is always something to learn in each situation. Whether you endured a tough relationship, bad job experience, or a hard life, accept the truth of the situation and move on. Instead of carrying the weight of the past or hiding behind painful events, feel the freedom of admitting a mistake and learning from it. The liberation of accepting it, then letting it go, does not make you weaker but stronger. Shakespeare wrote, *"Honesty is the best policy. If I lose my honor, I lose myself."* If your purpose is to get to where we should be or even come close to reaching your potential, build your future on the strength of truth.

Stepping up to take the blame for a mistake or to admit a fault takes extraordinary character. It also instills enormous confidence and courage as we move forward, because we know we have done the right thing. Regardless of the circumstances, always follow the truth wherever it may lead. Build your world on something solid and realize the power that comes from honesty. Margaret Lee Runbeck wrote, "*There is no power on earth more formidable than the truth.*" To build a foundation on falsehood or to live life in a state of denial will lead only to further problems. It creates borders and limits our potential—a painful or discouraging past that will be carried into the future. By being honest, there is no room for misconceptions, nothing to fear, and nothing to run from. The truth moves us powerfully forward. Lies are anchors that continually pull us back.

You can accomplish anything in life, any objective you put your mind to; but establish it on the truth. Sometimes it may take longer or be harder, but it will be genuine and invincible. If you want to return to school, start a different career, or embark on a new relationship, first be honest with yourself. Perhaps you had bad grades, did not really try, or did not study hard enough. Admit it, then improve on the past and become an academic. Maybe you had the wrong occupation or made bad decisions. Acknowledge it, then change your focus, adjust your strategy, and embark on a new career. Even in relationships, no one is blameless. To act faultless is weakness, but to understand where things went wrong and learn from them is magic. Goethe wrote, "*As soon as you trust yourself, you will know how to live.*" Honesty is the essential foundation on which to build the rest of your life. By basing everything on the truth, our opportunities are infinite.

# *The Truth of Victory*

*"Be prepared and be honest."* – John Wooden

John Robert Wooden was born in the small town of Hall, Indiana. Athletic and competitive as a child, he was destined for basketball. Starting at 14, he led his high school basketball team to the state championship finals for three consecutive years, winning the tournament in 1927. He attended Purdue University and became a three-time All-American guard. When Wooden graduated college, he played professionally for several years and coached a few high school teams. Not until he accepted the position as head coach at UCLA did his legacy begin. In his 27-year tenure, he won 665 games in 27 seasons. Under his guidance, UCLA won ten NCAA National Championships in 12 years, seven in a row, a record unmatched by any other coach or college basketball team in history. In 1972, he received Sports Illustrated magazine's *Sportsman of the Year* award and is deemed one of the greatest leaders on and off the court. His remarkable success was based on some simple principles that every player had to learn. From his *seven point creed*, his first belief is, *"Be true to yourself."* Wooden believed that regardless of your ability or skill, everything starts by being honest with yourself and others. Regardless of strategy or points on the board, if you did not give your best each game, then you lost. If you made excuses or blamed others, then you failed. The game was never about just winning, but by being real with your own ability and how hard you tried. He said, *"Don't measure yourself by what you have accomplished, but by what you should have accomplished with your ability."* It was from this foundation that Wooden not only inspired his team, but was able to get the best out of each player.

# *Facing the Truth*

## Key Concepts and Focus

- We always need to be honest with ourselves and others.
- The truth moves us powerfully forward. Lies are anchors that continually pull us back.
- Total honesty eradicates misconceptions and fear, leaving nothing to run from.
- Feel the freedom of admitting a mistake, learning from an event, then letting it go.
- Admit where you have been wrong, so you can learn how to be right.
- With the truth, you can build a solid foundation for the rest of your life.

# 26

## *You Are What You Eat*

*"One should eat to live, not live to eat."* - Cicero

Is there anything more important than properly taking care of our bodies? It takes great motivation and strength to be at our best and accomplish what we want. We cannot afford to undermine our daily performance by skipping meals or eating inadequately. Eating right is necessary for a healthy and well balanced life. One of the easiest ways to increase our energy and feel better is having a proper diet. With the right attitude and will, it is not that difficult. So many problems derive from a poor diet: fatigue, illness, moodiness, depression, loss of energy, inconsistent behavior, and excessive weight. Digestion alone uses over 60 percent of the body's energy. Therefore, if we are not consistently eating correctly, more energy is lost through this process. Master your diet, and you can master your life. It is not about complex or expensive products, for everything we require is simple and easily available. We just need to spend the time and focus on what we eat and how often.

Eating three balanced meals a day, but smaller portions, is essential. Skipping breakfast or a meal usually does not lead to weight loss. The body simply conserves its fat and burns muscle. Consistently eating right will increase our metabolism and burn more calories. Have a solid breakfast, mid-morning snack, a solid lunch, late afternoon snack, and a smaller dinner (not after 6:00 PM if possible). The body will burn about 70% of calories within the first part of the day; the other 30% happens over the course of the evening and into the night, so having a large dinner or eating late increases the chances of gaining weight and digestive problems.

Breakfast is the most important meal of the day. Wolfing down a muffin or eating some quick fast food product will only hurt your daily performance and cause future problems. Spend a few minutes preparing and eating a balanced meal. It is easy and quick. For breakfast, have some fruit with a high fiber cereal and two percent milk. Grab a few slices of 12-grain bread with honey. Oatmeal is good, but make sure to include fruit or nuts. Shakes are an excellent way to start the day and get the proper nutrition. Use a natural juice or two percent milk, a few eggs, fresh fruit, low-fat yogurt, and either a soy or whey protein powder. Do this three times a week and balance the other times with cereal, you will notice how much better you feel and how much more energy you have. Always eat a solid lunch, balanced with the needed food groups. Proper snacks in between meals helps provide consistent energy and reduces the amount you eat at the main meals. Take a multi-vitamin every day to supplement your dietary requirements.

### The Four Basic Food Groups
1.   Milk products: cheese, milk, yogurt, and ice cream
2.   Meat/eggs: red meats, poultry, fish and eggs
3.   Grains: breads, cereals, rice, pasta

4.   Fruits/vegetables: can be consumed as solids or juices

Finding the proper balance is key: 20 percent of a healthy diet should consist of milk, meat, and eggs, and 80 percent should be vegetables, fruits, and grains. All meals should contain fruits or vegetables, as well as grains. Meat or milk should be included in two of the meals. We also need adequate iron in our diets, found in fish and poultry. Try to avoid butter, excessive salt, and deserts. The best foods to consume before prolonged exercise are complex carbohydrates, which include pasta, potatoes, and rice.

### A Simple Time Table
- 6-8:00 A.M.: Breakfast—oatmeal, Bran cereal, shake (banana, protein powder, juice)
- 10:00 A.M.: Snack—yogurt, nuts, raisins, fruit
- 12:00-1:00 P.M. Lunch—sandwich (12-grain bread, turkey) and fruit/vegetable
- 3-4:00 P.M. Snack—yogurt, nuts, raisins, fruit
- 6:00 P.M. Dinner—chicken or fish, rice or pasta, with vegetables and milk

- Some General Diet Items:
    o   Fresh fruit (bananas, apples, blueberries)
    o   Fresh Vegetables (broccoli, green bean, peas, carrots)
    o   Brown rice and pasta
    o   Sliced turkey pastrami/chicken/turkey
    o   Tuna fish
    o   12-grain bread
    o   2 percent milk or soy milk
    o   Honey
    o   Peanuts (almonds), raisins

Taking the time to eat right is not about sacrifice. It is about doing what is required for a healthy life, maximizing our potential, and preparing for the future. Eating consistently balanced meals will increase energy, strength, and motivation. Expect to feel better. Always seize the opportunity for fresh fish and vegetables. Remember to eat smaller portions and have healthy snacks throughout the day. Break the bad habits of yesterday and start on a solid program today.

## *You Are What You Eat*

### Key Concepts and Focus

- Eating right is necessary for a healthy and well-balanced life.
- There are no excuses for a poor diet or bad habits.
- Eating right can provide more strength, stability and change our lives.
- Create a well-balanced plan and routine for your life.
- It is easy to eat well and feel better.

# 27

# *The Necessity of Physical Activity*

*"True enjoyment comes from activity of the
mind and exercise of the body; the two are
united."* – Alexander von Humboldt

One of the most important elements of a healthy, energetic, and
driven life is physical activity. Whether you enjoy working out
or not, it is vital for maximum achievement in everything we do.
Regular and consistent aerobic activity increases your fitness
level; stimulates blood circulation to your mind and body;
improves your mental ability; prevents cardiovascular disease;
reduces heart problems; lowers blood pressure; improves
flexibility; decreases stress; increases muscular strength and
endurance; builds healthy bones and joints; helps the heart work
more efficiently during the day and when sleeping, and controls
obesity by keeping unnecessary weight off, allowing the body to
adjust to its correct equilibrium.

Physical activity also helps us psychologically and
improves mental health. It reduces feelings of depression
and anxiety, improves our mood, and promotes a sense of
well-being. Those who work out regularly have more self-
esteem, increased ability to perform daily activities, higher
levels of alertness, and the aptitude to learn and retain more

information. In brain research and cognitive performance, working out is essential for the improvement of the mind. Exercise stimulates blood to the brain and allows it to work more efficiently. It improves brain function and protects against cognitive decline. These findings are similar in both young people and adults.

> For the best results, one should be working out at least five times a week for a minimum of 30-45 minutes. The mornings are the best time, for it sets the rhythm of the body and stimulates the mind. Using a scale between 1 and 10, the level of intensity and difficulty should be a 7 or higher. For maximum benefits, perform any moderate-to-vigorous-intensity activity at 50-85 percent of your maximum heart rate. If you are physically active for longer periods or at greater intensity, you will benefit more. It is best to confer with a professional trainer to set yourself up on the right program, understand the proper intensity, and learn how to get the most from each exercise. Some examples of activities that increase endurance and help the body are: aerobics, jogging, bicycling, cross-country skiing, dancing, martial arts training, rowing, swimming, tennis, and other sports. A simple method to follow is The FIT Formula:
>
> F = frequency (days per week)
> I = intensity (how hard/vigorous) % of heart rate
> T = time (amount for each session)

In setting up a routine, cross-training the body and muscles is a must. This means working your lower body one day and upper body the next. It also involves incorporating various activities. Using weights and machines is good, but also include other activities or sports, such as running, swimming, or tennis. The workouts should gradually increase in the amount of weight, length, and intensity for about three months. Then a new program should be started because your muscles become used to the regularity of the exercise and need to be challenged in a different way. A local club usually offers everything you need, but also get involved with a group activity, such as soccer, basketball, tennis, or racquetball. Disciplined and consistent physical activity will increase your energy, drive, and enthusiasm for life. It will help reduce stress, increase your mental capacity, and help you enjoy life to its fullest.

## *The Necessity of Physical Activity*

### Key Concepts and Focus

- One of the most basic fundamentals for a healthy, energetic, and driven life is physical activity.
- Exercise not only helps the body, but strengthens the mind.
- Make no excuses. Just start a good program today and stay with it.
- Find a good club and someone to help you set up a solid routine.
- Get involved in other sports, and always stay active.

*"Go as far as you can see; when you get there you'll be able to see farther"*
- Thomas Carlyle

# It's Not Just Another Dream
# If You Make It Real

*To have faith, when others lose theirs;*
*To act with integrity, even when confidence is gone;*
*To improve and grow daily, never falling back*
*To realize dreams when others only have wishes;*

*To see the potential in people, no their faults;*
*To forget other's failures and only see the good;*
*To always give without a desire for return;*
*To open your heart without the fear of hurt;*

*To understand, even when words are not spoken;*
*To have strength, even though weakness prevails;*
*To never stop believing, even though others doubt;*
*To dictate to life, not have life dictate to you;*

*To have a great vision, when everyone else is blind*
*To find your true calling and embrace it forever;*
*To see the possibilities, not the excuses*
*That is the true beginning of life.*

**Your New Beginning**

# *Workbook and Action Plans*

The workbook is designed to help you organize your thoughts, write down ideas, list goals, and create action plans for improvement and success. Thoroughly address each area, think about the questions, and write specific answers. The information, questions, and exercises will take time. As you list activities and objectives, make sure to complete something every day. If you want to improve or succeed, it takes dedication and commitment. The more you work on each section or goal, the better and faster the results.

## Step I: The Beginning
1) Take the initiative and get things moving.
2) Organize your time.
3) Schedule what needs to be done.
4) Once you have finished, review your lists and goals every morning and at night.

By focusing on these areas, ideas will surface and opportunities will appear. The more committed and organized you are, the stronger the outcome. You will need a separate pad of lined paper, a calendar, and eventually a computer. I have provided a place to write down some of the answers, but feel free to write more on a separate piece of paper or start a Word document on your computer.  Once this information is on your computer, you can add to it and update it regularly.

The workbook is only the beginning.  Improvement and personal development is a life-long journey and should never cease.

## Step II: Working Toward Your Goals
1) Always challenge yourself.
2) Continually read.  There are many books, CDs, and programs out there that can also enhance your life.
3) Travel and experience as much as you can.
4) Learn something new every day.
5) Find a friend or associate with whom you can share your goals and ambitions.
6) Seek out someone to participate in a sport, activity, or other pursuits in which you are interested.
7) If possible, work with a professional trainer and/or coach who will keep you accountable and push you to excel.
8) Whatever you do, never compromise.  Either do it well or not at all.
9) Start every goal with the intention of finishing it, and stay with it until it is realized.

## Step III: Action Plan
1) Organize a list of activities designed for the completion of a goal.
2) List ideas, thoughts, and objectives that help you achieve what you want.
3) Write down everything you need to do, what makes logical sense or is required to achieve success.

4) Spend fifteen-to-twenty minutes a day brainstorming. You will be surprised how much you can come up with in that short amount of time.

5) Work on it weekly to add other ideas, suggestions, and insights that come to mind during that week.

6) Add to the list and check off everything you have completed, such as phone calls made, research completed, people you met, or a book you read.

7) Create a Word document on your computer, so you are organized and can easily update a goal or category.

8) Start out by listing power points under each topic (a sentence for each idea or need).

9) Arrange them in the order you will complete them. Example: If losing weight is your goal, you could list:

**Losing 10 pounds in two months: (Date)**
- Ask someone who has done it and what worked.
- Talk to a professional trainer about your objectives.
- Join a gym or club.
- Find a good nutritionist and create a proper diet.
- Buy a recommended book to give you insight.
- Get the proper athletic gear.
- Organize a daily workout routine.
- Set a time frame and schedule for your goal.
- Start working out and training.
- Get a friend involved.
- Most critical of all is sticking with it.

Your action plans will be personalized to your specific needs. Each day, attack your lists and do as many things as you can. Stay focused and committed. The more you do, the easier the routine becomes. If properly done, you will soon see results and be able to build on them. Building momentum is key.

### Step IV: Following a Working Model

1) Do not try to reinvent the wheel or start at the beginning. Look for a good model or system that already works.
2) If you know people who have achieved great success, no matter the field, find out how they accomplished it.
3) Examine the methods they used and the steps they took.
4) Find a system or technique among the many out there that works well to fit your objectives. You can often consolidate ten years into a year by modeling another style, approach, or best practices.
5) Follow along these steps and make the proper adjustments.
6) Read biographies of professional or business people in whom you are interested.
7) Avoid their mistakes by focusing on their positive results.
8) Incorporate new ideas into your action plan and goals.

**Visualization:** Seeing something before it happens. Consciously and subconsciously, we have all practiced this technique. Perhaps it was thinking about a career, preparing for an event, or seeing a place we wanted to be. Visualization is one of the most powerful methods for accomplishing goals and succeeding. The more you focus on the objective and continually rehearse it, the easier and quicker the outcome. It programs your mind with the results you desire and helps guide you there. Famous speakers will repeatedly run through a speech in their mind before a presentation, great athletes visualize their performance before a game, and successful people see the outcome they want before it happens. The only difference is practicing something mentally instead of physically. Mental images can act as a prelude to muscular impulses and keeps your mind alert to recurring possibilities and opportunities. You can achieve any realistic goal if you keep on thinking about it, and eliminate any negative thoughts.

**Section 1:**

With all the following sections, you must follow through with what you list and the new action plans you create. Diligence and momentum are essential. Although you can change your life in an instant, with just one thought or determined idea, many of your objectives will take time, practice, and discipline. Stay with it. Continually review your goals, and develop longevity for your life. There is power and strength in repetition and action. Time is always moving; how we spend that time is what counts.

**Note:** With each question, you may want to use a separate note pad to elaborate on your answers.

## *Appreciate What You Have*

**Make a list of 10 things you are grateful for:**

_____

_____

_____

_____

_____

_____

_____

_____

_____

_____

Continually reflect on this list, and try to add at least a few things daily. By focusing on what we are grateful for, we create the capacity to receive more. This perspective improves our daily outlook and attitude for life.  Being thankful for what we have never takes away from what we want.  It just makes us more receptive for any future goals to which we aspire.  It also improves our awareness and inspires us to do more.

# *Your Childhood*

What where your goals when you were young?  What were your hopes and aspirations?

_____

_____

_____

_____

_____

Is there anything from this list that you still want to do or accomplish?

_____

_____

_____

_____

What action can you take now to pursue these areas?

***Your Action Plan**!*
- _____
- _____
- _____
- _____

This section is important, because we tend to lose our childlike faith, the excitement for life and attitude that anything is possible. By reflecting for a few moments, it is insightful to see what you may come up with.  Perhaps you wanted to be an artist, musician, athlete, or actor. You can still accomplish these goals. It may not be a fulltime profession, but you can start today to go after something you really wanted or still desire.

> **Example**: Buy some painting supplies and take an art class; purchase an instrument, take lessons, join a local band; start working out, hire a personal trainer, and join a neighborhood team; take some acting classes and audition for local theater productions. Getting involved in the things we love and the pursuits that bring us joy is essential. Do what you love and return to what you enjoy; an unfulfilled life is an empty one. One never knows where this can lead.

## *Your Education*

We should always remain students of life, and never stop learning. Education is important for our continued development and growth. It is never too late to master a skill or acquire new talents. Imagine what you can accomplish in just a few months or a year; how you can become proficient in a specific area or an expert in something you enjoy. Whether you are interested in a topic, subject or getting another degree, start today and learn something new.

List the subjects you are interested in learning or pursuing:

_____

_____

_____

_____

_____

Which one is the most important to you?

_____

What can you do now (today) to start pursing this subject? (Examples: college courses/program, books, CDs/DVDs, a tutor, local classes)

***Your Action Plan!***
- _____
- _____
- _____
- _____
- _____

## *Your Hobbies*

Regardless of your hectic work schedule or busy family life, relaxation and extracurricular activity is crucial to your weekly routine. Everyone needs time to rest and have fun. A well-balanced life helps us reflect, recharge, and enjoy what we do. Make sure you spend the proper time on this and incorporate it weekly.

List everything you enjoy doing:
(Sports, Recreation, Fun/entertainment)

_____

_____

_____

_____

_____

List what you would like to get involved with now:

_____
_____
_____
_____
_____

List the steps you can take today and schedule time on your calendar:
(Examples: call a friend, join a club, get involve with a team)

**Your Action Plan!**

- _____
- _____
- _____
- _____
- _____

# *Ways to Relax*

What do you do to relax?

_____
_____
_____
_____
_____

What could you be doing at least a few times a week for relaxation?

*Your Action Plan*!

- _____
- _____
- _____
- _____
- _____

# *Success and Career*

Our career or profession consumes most of our time and focus. We should enjoy and excel at what we do. Having the proper attitude and passion will fulfill your needs, provide prosperity, and foster success. Be clear about what you want and specific with your objectives.

What do you like about your profession?

_____
_____
_____
_____
_____

How can you enhance these areas? In what ways can you improve or build on them?

*Your Action Plan*!

- _____
- _____
- _____
- _____
- _____

What would you like to change and how?

(Is there someone to talk to; perhaps another division or position available?)

***Your Action Plan*!**

- _____
- _____
- _____
- _____
- _____

What professional skills are holding you back?
(Public speaking, business savvy, technical proficiency, communication)

_____

_____

_____

_____

_____

What do others say you need to improve?
(You can always ask colleagues for their insight)

_____

_____

_____

_____

_____

What areas or skills should you now change and develop?
(Get advice, take a class, sign up for a course)

***Your Action Plan*!**

- _____
- _____
- _____

- _____
- _____

List a few of the best managers you every worked for and why?

_____
_____
_____
_____
_____

What were their attributes you admired?
(Style, communication, mentoring, leadership, professionalism)

_____
_____
_____
_____
_____

Which characteristics can you incorporate to improve your own career?
(Modeling another style or technique that works is one of the best ways for improvement)

_____
_____
_____
_____
_____

What is the next step in your career? Where do you really want to go?

_____
_____

_____
_____
_____

What can you do to get there?
(Needed skills/experience, current opportunities, create a new resume, talk to your colleagues/boss)

*Your Action Plan*!

- _____
- _____
- _____
- _____
- _____

What is your ultimate professional goal?  Where do you see yourself in 15-20 years?
(Although this may be a difficult question, take time to think about it and write down a thorough answer)

_____
_____
_____
_____
_____

What is needed to make this a reality?
(Make a list of the practical steps and activities needed along the way)

*Your Action Plan*!

- _____
- _____
- _____
- _____
- _____

# *Personal Success*

List at least 5 answers for each section. Be as specific as possible.

When have you felt most alive and happy?

_____

_____

_____

_____

_____

What are you passionate about?

_____

_____

_____

_____

_____

What do you love to do?

_____

_____

_____

_____

_____

What brings you the greatest joy in life?

_____

_____

_____

_____

_____

When do you feel at your best?

_____

_____

_____

_____

_____

What are your natural talents?

_____

_____

_____

_____

_____

What are your best skills?

_____

_____

_____

_____

_____

What are your personal strengths and characteristics?

_____

_____

_____

_____

_____

What have others always said that you are good at?

_____

_____

_____

_____

_____

If you could do anything, what would it be?

_____

_____

_____

_____

_____

What do these answers have in common?

_____

_____

_____

_____

_____

In the previous questions, you should find common characteristics. Your answers should help guide you in realizing or discovering what you really want out of life, what career you should pursue or activities you should be involved with.

## *Personal Mission Statement*

Next, craft a personal mission statement for your life. This statement will represent who you are and what you truly want to become. Review and reflect on this daily. Open up your mind and discuss the possibilities that already exist. Start to become aware of ideas and opportunities as they present themselves.

_____
_____
_____
_____
_____
_____
_____
_____
_____

# *Beliefs*

Every decision we make in life is based on our beliefs. Influenced by our past experiences and perceptions, they define and dictate our attitude. Every conversation, relationship, and situation is measured and justified by what we believe. Our expectations, personality, and how we treat others derive from this mindset. Many beliefs are inspiring and move us forward, while others are incapacitating and limit everything we do. Often based on generalizations and misconceptions, they undermine our behavior and the decisions we make.

What beliefs are hindering you and holding you back from accomplishing more?
(Negative beliefs that have manifested through the years)

_____
_____
_____

_____

_____

Why do you believe these things?  What has led you to these conclusions?
(Repeated bad experiences, unkind words, misconceptions)

_____

_____

_____

_____

_____

Do you truly feel that these beliefs are correct, or can you change some of them in order to improve your life?  List some new proactive solutions and actions you will take to improve. Every time you are in a situation that challenges your changed perspective, rehearse these new thoughts and frequently take action.  This repetition helps reprogram your mind, break old patterns, and forms positive habits.

**Past Belief**                                **New Action**

_____  →  _____

_____  →  _____

_____  →  _____

_____  →  _____

_____  →  _____

## *Excuses*

Excuses compromise life and keep us from doing what we want. They distract us from obligations and goals.  Take responsibilities for your actions. What excuses are you using that keep you from accomplishing more? List at least five:

_____

_____

_____

_____

_____

What can you now do to replace each excuse with a proactive action?

**Excuse**                          **New Action**

_____ → _____

_____ → _____

_____ → _____

_____ → _____

_____ → _____

# *Words*

Words have the power either to inspire or discourage, to motivate or debilitate. They have a profound effect on our attitude and behavior. They form obstacles in our mind and lead to discouragement. Half the words we use in our vocabulary are negative. List ten negative words you always use and replace them with positive ones. Become aware of their recurrence in your daily thoughts and conversations. When a negative idea or expression enters your mind, quickly replace it with a positive one. This is a mental exercise in reprogramming your thoughts that works. It will take time at first, but the more you do this, the easier it becomes.

Example: hate→love, never→possible,
too late→still feasible, failure→temporary setback,
impossible→attainable

| Negative Word | | Positive Word |
|---|---|---|
| _____ | → | _____ |
| _____ | → | _____ |
| _____ | → | _____ |
| _____ | → | _____ |
| _____ | → | _____ |
| _____ | → | _____ |
| _____ | → | _____ |
| _____ | → | _____ |
| _____ | → | _____ |
| _____ | → | _____ |

## *Negative Habits*

List 3-4 areas or habits you would like to improve or change:

_____

_____

_____

_____

_____

For each answer, list 5-10 reasons why you want to improve or
eliminate these areas, vices or problems.

_____

_____

_____

_____

_____

_____

_____

_____

_____

_____

_____

Always focus on the *why*. This justifies your reason for getting better and improving. It supports your intentions and motivates your mind into action. Stay focused on the results you want, not the habits you are trying to improve. Whenever a negative urge or desire resurfaces, remember why you want to stop.

What action steps can you take to improve or eliminate these areas? Perhaps you can replace the urge to smoke, eat, or drink with something else. Maybe take a walk, work out, throw out all the bad food in the house, or listen to music for few minutes to stimulate your mind and break your old patterns.

### *Your Action Plan!*

- _____
- _____
- _____
- _____
- _____

# *Important Focus*

What are 10 things you believe to be important in life?

_____

_____

_____

_____

_____

_____

_____

_____

_____

_____

What is the most important thing to you?

_____

_____

_____

How is this belief incorporated into your daily life? What are you doing to reinforce this belief? Maybe you need to change something or get away from a negative situation to foster positive results.

# *Your Goals*

### Section 2: Goals

Goals are the maps that represent our ambitions and desires for the future. If we do not create goals, they will never become realities. If you do not see it, you cannot have it. Too often we limit ourselves by not clearly articulating what we want. Anything in life is possible, but we have to take the initiative to make it happen. If we aim high, we hit high; aim low, and that is where we end up. The more specific your goal is, the better the outcome.

Once you form a list, mentally and emotionally connect with each one. Focus on the end result and visualize what it would be like to have it. Once you powerfully connect with something, there is little that can stop it. It may not come instantly, and some goals will take years to accomplish; but the more focused and determined you are, the closer it becomes. This is a simple law of nature and a powerful way to change your life.

List every goal you have for your entire life. Try to write at least 100. Whatever goals you listed prior, you can incorporate them now. These goals can be anything you want, such as a new car, house, relationship, marriage, children, money, wealth, trips, items, anything and everything; there is no limit. Do not holdback your answers.

Have fun writing out everything you can come up with. (You may need a larger sheet of paper).

**Your 100 Goals**

| | | |
|---|---|---|
| _____ | _____ | _____ |
| _____ | _____ | _____ |
| _____ | _____ | _____ |
| _____ | _____ | _____ |
| _____ | _____ | _____ |
| _____ | _____ | _____ |
| _____ | _____ | _____ |
| _____ | _____ | _____ |
| _____ | _____ | _____ |

_____    _____    _____

_____    _____    _____

_____    _____    _____

When you are done, organize each answer in a specific area below:

1.  Personal Development and Education
2.  Career and Profession
3.  Health and Body

4.   Relationships
5.   Recreation and Travel
6.   Financial and Wealth

Organize each goal in the order of importance, rating it on a scale between 1 and 10.

Next, define the timeframe of these goals (1-20 years). When would you like to complete each one?

Once you have completed the exercises, choose 2 or 3 of the most important goals from each section in the one-year time frame. Write a small paragraph explaining why you want each goal. This helps you connect clearly with them, defining your intention and purpose. Your answers do not need to be profound or involved. Just know why you want each one.

These 12-15 goals will be your specific areas of focus for the next year. Put a date at the top of each one, so you know the exact time you started your plan. You can start an action plan for your life anytime. Your New Year starts with the date you add. The next step is to form an action plan for each one year goal.

**Action Plans:**
Outline an action plan for each goal you chose, and list everything you can do to accomplish it. Brainstorm, and think of anything that is needed. Start with small and manageable tasks, so you can complete them and build momentum. Other areas may take weeks or months to complete, but just stay consistent each day. The more time you commit to your goals, the more you will get done, experience, and discover.

**Action Plan Example:** *Find a new job*

- Make a list of what you want to do:
    - What positions are you interested in?
    - What would be the most fulfilling role or job?
- Create a new resume:
    - Research other resumes online and pick the proper format.
    - Go through every section and clearly articulate your skills and experience.
    - Work with a friend or associate to help you brainstorm.
    - Ask someone to proofread the resume, and get constructive feedback.
    - If possible, hire a professional resume writer.
- Write a letter of introduction:
    - Have someone proofread it.
- Research the industry you are interested in:
    - Pick 25-50 companies you want to work for.
    - Read through the highlights of each company, and see what opportunities are available.
    - Send at least 2 or 3 resumes a day to different companies.
    - Keep a separate list of companies, emails, and phone numbers to review and continually contact.
- Spend a few hours each week rehearsing your resume for future interviews:
    - Go through each area so you are ready and polished for an interview.
- Start networking with friends and associates:
    - Meet with at least 1 or 2 people a week to discuss opportunities.
    - Join local network groups or clubs.

This is just an example of an action plan for a goal. Your action plans can be comprehensive or simple, whatever works for you. The idea is to get focused and move in the direction you want; to do something every day and build momentum. Be as precise as you can and put them in the order that you want to complete. Use a calendar and plan specific times (at least one hour per day) for the different tasks. The more you work on it, other ideas will come.

## *Successful Traits and Principles*

- **Energy**
  - o Most successful people maintain a high level of great physical and intellectual energy, working in unison. Athletic fitness, a good diet, and proper rest are essential. Make the most of your gifts and talents by staying healthy and alert.
- **Passion**
  - o Passion is that inner force that drives us forward and motivates results. It provides us with the enthusiasm and power to endure setbacks and move forward. Do what you enjoy and are passionate about.
- **Integrity**
  - o Integrity involves honesty and consistency in everything we do. Never compromise your beliefs and stay true to what you value. Treat others with respect and compassion.
- **Positive Attitude**
  - o Stay focused and optimistic. Look for the good in each event or what can be learned. If you focus on the negative, you become negative and draw more of this into your life. If you maintain a positive attitude, you are inspired to do more and work harder.
- **Confidence**
  - o If you do not believe in yourself, others will not believe in you. Connect with your desires and have certainty you will achieve them. Never waiver from an inspired idea or allow difficult circumstances to dictate to you. Make success a dominate thought and never get distracted

or discouraged with obstacles or problems. Be confident and continually move forward.

- **Vision**
    - Have far-reaching goals that push you to excel and use all of your abilities. Never limit what you can accomplish. Trust your instincts and see what is possible.
- **Communication Skills**
    - Be clear in conveying your thoughts and messages. Frequently communicate with others about your expectations or needs. Be an effective listener as well as communicator.
- **Strategy**
    - Create a specific plan to accomplish your goals and objectives. Stay consistent and adapt to changes. Organize your resources, skills, and opportunities to gain results effectively.
- **Willingness to Learn**
    - Be willing to ask questions and learn everything you can about a subject. Always be inquisitive, read continually, write down new information, and review what you learn.
- **Taking Risks**
    - Those who succeed are not afraid to take risks. They are willing to fail or do whatever it takes to learn and grow forward. Be willing to make mistakes and take chances. If you always wait for everything to be perfect, you will always be waiting.
- **Leadership**
    - If people do not respect you, they will not follow you. Communicate clearly and bring out the best in others. Productively organize your thoughts and objectives into a powerful and clear strategy. Lead by example. Be proactive and make the necessary decisions. Stand behind what you do and always follow through.
- **Relaxation**
    - Proper balance is crucial for success. You never want to burn out or become overwhelmed with

exhaustion. Spend time relaxing. Do things that are fun and give you time to rest and reset. Relaxation helps you clear your mind and be ready for tomorrow.

- **Giving and Receiving**
    - o  You must be willing to give to receive. Those who succeed always give back to others, whether guidance, help, time, or money.

*What lies behind you and what lies in front of you, pales in comparison to what lies inside you*
                    - Emerson